G000152027

A FOODIE AFLOAT

To
Tam, Kathleen and Kay

They made this book
The mistakes are mine

A FOODIE AFLOAT

A cook's journey through France on a barge. A secret world of canals and rivers.
An enticing story of slow boats, slow food, small events and chance encounters

Di Murrell

Cover Design and Illustrations

by Kathleen Caddick

Copyright © 2020 Di Murrell
Cover design and illustrations by Kathleen Caddick
Cover photographs by Tam and Di Murrell

The moral right of the author has been asserted.

Apart from any fair dealing for the purposes of research or private study,
or criticism or review, as permitted under the Copyright, Designs and Patents
Act 1988, this publication may only be reproduced, stored or transmitted, in
any form or by any means, with the prior permission in writing of the
publishers, or in the case of reprographic reproduction in accordance with
the terms of licences issued by the Copyright Licensing Agency. Enquiries
concerning reproduction outside those terms should be sent to the publishers.

Matador
9 Priory Business Park,
Wistow Road, Kibworth Beauchamp,
Leicestershire. LE8 0RX
Tel: 0116 279 2299
Email: books@troubador.co.uk
Web: www.troubador.co.uk/matador
Twitter: @matadorbooks

ISBN 978 1838593 513

British Library Cataloguing in Publication Data.
A catalogue record for this book is available from the British Library.

Printed and bound by CPI Group (UK) Ltd, Croydon, CR0 4YY

Matador is an imprint of Troubador Publishing Ltd

CONTENTS

RECIPES

12 It's Quicker by Car

INTRODUCTION

Although not without the odd moment of high drama, voyages in our barge *Friesland* hardly equate to the swashbuckling adventures of sailors on the high seas. We just potter along quiet canals and meandering rivers, climbing hillsides lock by lock, passing through shady cuttings and dank tunnels on the high summit levels, then dropping down into the next valley through yet more locks, eventually to be disgorged into a river whose name we probably do not even know.

We have spent the last twenty years on the waterways of mainland Europe, usually in France with occasional forays into Belgium, the Netherlands and Germany. The boating is full of contrasts: whole days spent negotiating flights of locks on a small canal in the pouring rain; misty mornings and breezy afternoons keeping track of the buoys which mark the channel on some great river. When necessary, there are early starts in winter darkness, steel deck heavily frosted with me 'the crew' in sleepy sullen mood untying icily unyielding mooring lines. Occasionally we will find ourselves still on the move well into the evening, looking for somewhere, anywhere, to stop for the night out of the wash of the huge barges thundering by. Why do we do it? Because even when it's awful, it's great. And there are always those long lazy days of summer to look forward to – memories of which fuel this infatuation with the barging life throughout the long wintertime.

Dismissed as 'ditch crawlers' by intrepid sailors, I, nevertheless, love the sedate way in which we negotiate the landscape. For us, this is a journey without a final destination; it is simply a journey waymarked by the people we meet and defined by the food and drink we discover en route. We see life, as it were, through the back door of whichever country we are in. How else could we engage in the companionable, albeit brief, exchange of words with that old fellow in his canal-side garden as he hoes between his rows of vegetables or with those guys paddling about in the muddy shallows collecting freshwater crayfish in a bucket as we go boating by?

We are the willing recipients of canal-side largesse: lock-keepers offer their garden produce, pointing me down the path to where the best beans, tomatoes or lettuces are to be found. From one we have bought jars of truffles collected from the forest close to his back door; apple eau de vie from another made with his own apples and turned into a spirituous brew by the last of the roving distillers who stops by every year; from others we have happily accepted gifts of over-sized courgettes, sacks of pears and plums and once three freshly laid goose eggs.

To spend one night cocooned in the velvet darkness of the countryside far from any dwelling and the next to lie exposed and vulnerable under incandescent lights at the centre of a bustling city, offers contrasts not to be found in any other form of modern travel. Nor do we need to be searching always for somewhere new to visit. We look forward to returning to familiar places, each with some special attribute of its own;

it may be just the one thing they make really well, like the boudin blanc in Rethel on the Canal des Ardennes, the pâté en croûte from the bakers at Cumières on the River Marne or the wine bought from Alphonse Mellot's shop on the very top of the hill in Sancerre on the Canal du Centre. We know we can tie up on the doorstep of such places and will be welcome to stay as long as we like.

On our travels we stop to visit farms, smallholdings, gardens and orchards; shop for the region's specialities at the weekly markets; sample local dishes; visit the winemakers and check out the restaurants. We can buy our milk straight from the cow, cheese direct from the maker and foie gras from the lady who feeds the geese. We have the time to find out from the village butcher the best way to cook an unknown cut of meat and from the *charcutier* how to serve an unfamiliar dish on display in his window. We do not come as visitors with barely time to settle before moving on, but as residents, albeit in transit. For the time being our address will be wherever we choose to tie our barge, be it the village pontoon, some city quay, a deserted sand wharf on a river bank or that canal-side grain silo on the outskirts of town. Wherever we are, we are at home.

It's not all rusticity and bucolic living though. After all, canals were built as trade routes to serve the needs of agriculture and industry. We will find ourselves occasionally boating through the old industrial heartlands of France and Belgium. When these waterways are still serving the purpose for which they were originally built, we feel small and out of place as we pass beneath great cooling towers, staring wide-eyed up at the busy scrap and aggregates wharves, steelyards and smelting works. *Friesland* – 24 metres long and just over 4 metres wide – is quite big for a private boat, yet here in this environment, is utterly dwarfed by the enormous barges that come from all over Europe to discharge their freight of pressed scrap cars and to load again with the finished steel coils destined for Rotterdam or Antwerp. Sand barges progress majestically along the waterway, sometimes six or eight at a time, tied two abreast, propelled along by enormous pusher tugs with names like 'Nemesis' or 'Titanic'; we roll in their wake as they pass by.

Imperceptibly the rainbow laden oily water in which our barge is floating thins and, as in a film, a slow fade moves us from industrial murkiness into sunlight and a more sympathetic land, where quiet villages of fine stone houses, farmyards and barns dot the scene. Here chickens scratch in the dust, cats laze in the sunshine and old men and their dogs drowse in doorways of the lock cottages as we slip by. Mostly the old men stay put – they've seen it all before – but the dog will usually rouse himself and amble over, hoping some titbit will come his way. We rise in the lock, the dog peers down from above. Who can resist that hopeful look? By the time we are level I have a slice of sausage or biscuit ready. He takes the morsel offered, turns and ambles back to the doorway, content.

Vineyards sweep down the hillsides in impeccable rows like lines of soldiers on parade. In such places our days pass slowly; we too bask in the sun, then swing the boarding ladder over the side to swim in the clear water. On deck, in the cool of evening and over a glass of wine, we are entertained by the aerial dances of bats and swallows swooping low in search of their supper. Accompanying music supplied for free, courtesy of frogs and cicadas.

Eventually though we are ready to depart, off in search of more intellectual pursuits, more sophisticated suppers. Then *Friesland* must edge into graffiti covered suburbs and we begin to feel a little vulnerable – here be people.

Sometimes there is no choice but to continue on into the badlands where every group of young men hanging about close to a lock, lurking on the towpath or leaning over the parapets of the bridge through which we are passing, is viewed with trepidation. Then before you know it, we have arrived, fetching up in attractive and surprisingly peaceful surroundings in the middle of a city, often a mere stone's throw from some historic monument or architectural wonder. What visitor, other than he who arrives by water, can find himself congenially at home beneath the Eiffel Tower, beside the famous windmills of Bruges or in the middle of old Amsterdam?

We travel slowly, yes, but in the process discover more than any speeding motorist could ever hope to. We see places that no normal holidaymaker will ever visit and view them from an entirely different perspective. Not for us then the tourist trails and high-profile routes through the most popular parts. If we happen to find ourselves in such places it is by chance rather than intent. After all we can only go where the waterways we travel take us. Best of all when we do stop and tie up, local people do not view us with that suspicion reserved for unknown callers in out-of-the-way places. We are accepted simply as people who are passing through. On a boat. In fact, for the 'ditch crawlers' that we are.

This book is a distillation of our wanderings, taking place over a year or so, on the lesser-known waterways of central and northern France.

We are seasoned 'bargees' and therefore long past that stage where the boating is full of amusing mishaps and ill-judged escapades. We avoid mistakes as far as possible; we are careful and capable; we try never to run aground or fall off the boat! Even so, journeying by boat is essential to my story. For sure, one can get to almost any of the places I mention by road but it is only from the vantage point of the water that an encounter with a catcher of crayfish or a hunter of truffles becomes a proper adventure and worth recording, especially when it occurs by chance.

As a cook and a lover of good food I quite enjoy the constraints that the boating often imposes. We can only go where the canal or river we are on takes us, which may mean long days passing through a countryside of farmland, field and forest, where often the only habitation near to hand is the lock-keeper's cottage. I thrive on the slight but constant concern that we may not have enough on board for me to put together, each day, at least a couple of meals which are both sustaining and tasty. I enjoy being frugal and am content to shop in those small country markets meant only to provide local people with local produce. Sometimes limited choice calls for extra creativity and it's truly rewarding to turn those few ingredients into the simple yet appetising dishes of the region we find ourselves in. I like watching out for wild stuff growing and enjoy, as the seasons change, my forages along the towpath. I love being given things I would probably never normally eat, or to be able to buy for a few centimes, produce dug up on the spot from a waterside garden or allotment. Out in the French countryside food is familial and seasonal. I am very happy to go along with this though sometimes, when a touch homesick, I yearn for food with a distinctly British quality: a roasted joint; boiled bacon; a fried egg sarnie; crumpets and scones and, just occasionally, a full-on curry when my desire for those great big spicy mouthfuls becomes overwhelming. Nevertheless, I appreciate the refinement of classic French cooking and do, on occasion, try to emulate that too. And I love it when we arrive back in so-called 'civilisation': those chic cities where delicacies from all corners of the earth are to be found and chefs whose only purpose is to serve them to us in ever more fanciful form. Here we can moor up, in our own home, and be immediately absorbed into a world of culinary sophistication. Such contrasts: a peasant-like frugality driven by necessity on the one hand and occasional epicurean excess on the other are equally beguiling and create an absorbing eclectic mix.

So, taken altogether, I hope this book gives you a good illustration of my water-bound foodie adventure. One which you, dear reader, might care to share, albeit from the comfort of your kitchen chair

My journey begins in northern France in the town of Cambrai. Initially we head east to Strasbourg, approximately 120 boating hours away, via the St Quentin Canal, the Aisne-Marne Canal and the Marne-Rhine Canal. At Strasbourg we retrace our footsteps traveling back along the same waterways to Reims, the champagne capital of France. From there we turn south again, onto the Champagne-Burgundy Canal and head down to our winter mooring at Auxonne on the River Saône.

On inland waterways distance from place to place is measured in engine hours – that is the number of hours the engine is basically running in order for us to make the passage. A rough calculation of this particular year's journey time is about 500 engine hours. Generally when we are boating we mostly do around six to eight engine hours a day but if we find somewhere particularly congenial, we might stop there for several days, and sometimes for weeks at a time. Once, a brief stop to fill up tanks with drinking water turned into a year's sojourn.

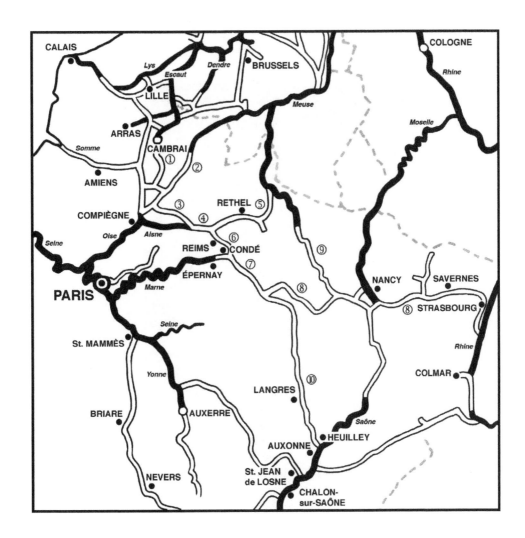

CANALS AND NAVIGABLE RIVERS
OF NORTH & CENTRAL FRANCE
Canals mentioned in the text:

① C. St Quentin   ② C. de la Sambre à l'Oise

③ C. de l'Oise à l'Aisne   ④ C. Latèral à l'Aisne

⑤ C. des Ardennes   ⑥ C. de l'Aisne à la Marne

⑦ C. Latèral à la Marne   ⑧ C. de la Marne au Rhin

⑨ C. de l'Est.   ⑩ Heuilley Canal   (C. entre Champagne et Bourgogne)

CHAPTER 1

Dear Old Cambrai

Inside *Friesland* it is freezing cold. Having had no heating on at all for several winter weeks whilst we have been dallying in London and with the Cantimpré basin at Cambrai in northern France, where the barge is moored, frozen solid, our first priority is to get her warmed up.

No problem – one flick of a switch and the diesel-fired boiler can be heard humming away down in her nether regions.

'It's up and running.'

'No, it's not.'

'It's stopped.'

Captain switches it on again.

'There – hear that hum?'

'It's up and running.'

'No, it's not.'

Oh dear. Standing here in the saloon in the freezing cold I've just remembered how much I hate barges. It is like being in charge of a small town. There's the heating, the water, the gas, the generator, the sewage and the electrics; then there are all those pumps and valves and pipes and switches, and that's before we even get to the bits you need to make the damned thing go: engines, rudders, propellors, anchors, thrusters, radios, depth-sounders and the like. Each and every one comes complete with its own built in supply of bloody-mindedness.

Captain goes off to peer at the boiler. It remains sullen and silent – resisting him. After a while, merely for want of something to do, he flicks the switch again and behold, it runs, it hums, and it begins to warm the boat. 'What was up then?' I ask when he returns. 'No idea,' he says, 'probably just bloody-mindedness.'

It is spring; early perhaps but still spring – everywhere else. Not in Cambrai though. Here it is still winter.

Back in England when we tell people we have a barge in France, they 'ooh' and they 'aah'. 'How lucky you are', 'What a wonderful life' – 'so warm and all that sunshine.' Little do they know that the sun never shines this close to Belgium. It is rarely warm and it rains a lot. Between the Russian Steppes and Cambrai there's not much cover and the glacial wind that howls across the icy vastness of northern Europe is heading just for here. It may be in France but you definitely would not come to Cambrai for the weather.

My mood improves as the heater continues working. My Captain has also beaten the loo pump into submission; our freshly made bed is full of hot water bottles and the beery beef casserole I made earlier, my tribute to the cooking of the north, and brought with us for supper is warming up nicely in the oven. I begin to view our return to Cambrai in a more positive light and spare a moment to contemplate its history.

The town is situated on the banks of the Escaut, which is, at this point, a mere stripling, giving no hint of its eventual emergence as one of the great rivers of northern Europe. At more than 400 kilometres in length, it first bubbles up into the light of day quite close to Cambrai; a truly Flemish waterway, crossing northern France and from thence passing into Belgium. Somewhere en route it begins a metamorphosis from gentle, unassuming little Escaut into the mighty Schelde, with Antwerp as its primary port. Leaving Belgium and meandering through the immense delta formed by the Zeeland islands, it finds its way into the Netherlands. Joined here by its two more famous sisters, the Meuse and the Rhine, all three finally lose themselves in the tidal waters of the North Sea.

Cambrai has always been an important trading centre and was once a member of the powerful Hanseatic League. Then, as now, grain was the town's mainstay and inside its mediaeval ramparts great warehouses stored its harvests. Today's grain, too large to be accommodated within the town, is contained in the silos that tower, cathedral like, over the prairie of wheat and sugar beet that encircles the town. Many of these silos are to be found on the banks of the surrounding waterways so that here in the north barges still regularly load and move thousands of tons of cereals. More often than not this will be barley for the Belgian beer industry or wheat for export to be loaded direct from the barges onto ships in the ports of Antwerp or Rotterdam. This smattering of working traffic still trading along the northern waterways adds an extra dimension to our boating; one which has been lost on the more southerly waterways where nowadays only pleasure craft are to be found.

The cuisine of Cambrai is very definitely of the north. Solid Flemish peasant food. It might take a while for a foreigner to truly appreciate many of the local dishes: tripe, calves head and chitterling sausage spring immediately to mind. They sound so much more desirable in French – tripes à la mode, tête de veau and andouillettes, but even so you may feel that this, the most robust of all French cooking, is food you need to have grown up with to truly enjoy. That's fine, though anyone visiting this area of France who does have a taste for liver, lights and the like is in for a bit of a treat.

Most famous of all the local specialities are the andouillettes. This is a chitterling sausage and as andouillettes go, those made in Cambrai are the most refined. The ones from the city of Troyes in the Champagne region, for instance, taste like a steaming farmyard midden with the cockerel still crowing from the top. Okay perhaps if you are a Trojan but a taste too far for the rest of us. Unlike the andouillettes from other regions which are made from the intestines of the pig, the Cambrai sausage is an altogether more delicate beast, its innards being from the stomach lining of calves.

The recipe and method of making this chitterling sausage is authenticated by the Association Amicale des Amateurs d'Authentique Adouillettes which is as much a mouthful as the thing itself. Surely this must be one of the most exclusive gastronomic societies in the world; membership is apparently limited to five. Who they are and how they are chosen I have no idea but each year a whole host of andouillettes get tasted and a diploma is awarded to the makers of the best. Just look for the stamp of the five 'A's' when you buy; it is the mark of the real McCoy. In fact just about every self-respecting restaurant in Cambrai has andouillettes on its menu, either flambéed using the local genever from Houlle or served with a grain mustard sauce. All I can say is, should you ever come this way, give andouillettes a chance.

Other local specialities like tarte Maroilles, potjevfleisch, leek flamiche and tarte au sucre may be easier to come to grips with. We love the beer braised beef or chicken casseroles topped with crisp spiced bread. Country pâtés made in this region are amongst the best in France and I have perfected a delicious way to cook that commonest of all the locally grown vegetables, the endive, which here you can buy by the kilo for less than a couple of euros.

The regions of Flanders, Picardy and the Artois don't show off too much about their culinary specialities. They may take a little time to track down but once found you are more than recompensed for your trouble. There is wonderful artisanal produce available from the many small farms, dairies, and market gardens dotted around Cambrai. Not easy to find though; often hidden away at the end of bumpy cobbled lanes or beside the dirt tracks that wind between the vast fields of sugar beet and grain. This is also a region that produces all those other solid and reliable staples of every day home cooking: onions, garlic, leeks, potatoes, cabbage, celeriac. We are always amazed at the incredible cheapness of the fruit and veg that can be bought at the farmer's door. I fantasise about how we could live really well on a mere handful of euros a week, eating nothing but potatoes and onions with an occasional ham hock thrown into the pot to liven things up. If times were to become seriously hard we could just hole up here, hatches battened down and live, oh so cheaply, on nothing but what we can buy within a kilometre or two of Cambrai. Given a bike and the boat, Armageddon and how to survive it begins to sound quite attractive. The only major drawback that I can immediately see is the lack of vinery. And the horrible weather. Local beer is pretty good though, as is the gin.

Cambrai's Saturday morning market is held in the town's stunningly ugly 1950s market house. First stall on the left as you head in through the main entrance is 'manned' by a family of lady chicken farmers. There are three generations behind the counter. Grandmother hovers in the background busily plucking and gutting our purchases. Mother and daughter serve the never-ending queue of regulars. They know everyone. There's time for a quick chat but the line is kept moving. This is always our first port of call, and we tag on to the end to buy the delicious pâté de foie they make, which is unquestionably, and especially when eaten with freshly wood-oven baked bread and my sweet and sour homemade pickled courgettes, our best Saturday lunch ever and one we have practically every weekend when we are in Cambrai,

In its season, there's a lady whose stall is piled so high with watercress she can barely see over the top. The fresh, peppery, crunchy bunches are the size of floral bouquets. When I see it marked at three bunches for a euro I can't resist. That's enough for several days of soups and salads and sandwiches.

In time, there will be any number of asparagus growers displaying their wares, which vary in size from the thinnest of sprue to stems the thickness of a giant's finger. There's a man at the far end of the hall who grows a whole variety of fresh herbs. From the surrounding countryside he collects wild ones too; rocket and marjoram, young nettle tops and dandelion leaves. His tiny earth-covered potatoes, steamed (after first removing the dirt) with fresh mint and eaten with a sprinkle of truffle-flavoured sea salt and a dollop of best butter would be a prime candidate for, were I ever to find myself there, my last supper on death row.

On their stalls the dairy farmers have unpasteurised milk, and crème fraîche as thick as clotted cream. Some make the Maroilles cheese, quite simply one of the great cheeses of France, while their wives are kept busy producing its wonderfully appetising byproduct – Tarte Maroilles. The base of this tart is like a savoury sponge; beautifully light and a perfect foil for the topping of rich and creamy cheese, which, after a few minutes reheating in a hot oven, becomes meltingly soft beneath its crispy brown bubbling surface.

The making of cambric and the weaving of tapestries, which once made Cambrai famous, no longer bring prosperity to the town. Today, for those few who have even heard of the place, it is forever associated with the staging, during the First World War, of the very first tank battle in history. Whilst there is a small but steady trickle of visitors who come to pay their respects to the dead of two world wars, this region, with Cambrai at its centre, is not somewhere that one would be drawn to as a holiday destination or even for a day out.

For the foreign inland boater though – by which I mean principally the Dutch, the Belgians and the British – Cambrai is a real haven. Heading into France by river and canal from further north or from the English Channel one has no choice but to travel long distances on the big and somewhat inhospitable commercial waterways, where craft of up to 180 metres in length and carrying thousands of tonnes of freight are the norm; having to pass at very close quarters and share locks with such monsters can be a daunting experience. It is surprising how many who arrive in Cambrai, somewhat shell-shocked from their first experience of commercial waterways, have set out on their small boats from the UK with no idea of the size and scale of the inland shipping that exists in this part of Europe. It therefore comes as a huge relief to those heading south to finally turn off onto the quiet St Quentin Canal, knowing that these locks can only accommodate one commercial vessel of no more 40 metres in length and that, therefore, those monsters out on the Grand Gabarit cannot follow them here.

Once onto the canal (which, more correctly at this point, is the canalised section of the River Escaut) and on up through half a dozen locks, Cambrai is the first town of any size that one comes to and here, once through the lock, a boat can turn off into the slightly rundown but not unwelcoming Port de Plaisance. There's a tap to replenish water tanks, electricity points to plug into and a local fuel supplier a mere telephone call away. The Café de la Marine is a friendly bar that takes in our mail and Le Petit Chef a quintessentially traditional French family run restaurant which stands barely yards from where we moor. With such services immediately to hand it is the ideal place to stop for a while, recharge both the boat's batteries and one's own and quietly recover from the unexpected rigours of those big waterways one never knew existed.

Over the years we have seen people arriving on their boats and barges vowing to go no further. Wives hightail it back to Britain declaring that the boating life is not for them; their old man lingers on in Cambrai scanning the internet in hopes of finding a more amenable crew so that his odyssey may continue. For others it is a mere hop and a skip to the Channel ports and home and thus a most convenient place to leave one's boat in the winter. And for some, providing they have a goodly supply of winter fuel, it's a convivial enough place to stay on board and ride out the seasonal storms. It's true that Cambrai seems, at first, much the same as any other knocked about northern French town with little to keep a casual visitor amused; it takes a while to appreciate just what is on offer. But there is a real warmth and friendliness about the place, a casual acceptance of our presence here and we feel a sense of security.

Perhaps it's the rich spicy aroma of our gently heating dinner that is triggering rosy memories of all the good times past spent in Cambrai; maybe it's the tentacles of cosy warmth that are at last spreading themselves throughout the boat and inducing that soporific state of semi-hibernation one associates with very cold weather and barges; or it may just all be down to the powerful pre-prandial of Belgian beer I am enjoying and which seems so much more appropriate than wine up here in the north. Whatever ... the ranting virago from earlier in the day has been replaced by a benign old dear hugging beer to bosom while tripping off down memory lane.

RECIPES

A regional product made locally and bought from a good *charcuterie* or a market stall has been made by experts and is likely to be cheaper and definitely better than anything I could make from scratch. So wait until you visit northern France to sample the Tarte Maroilles, the pâté de foie or the andouillettes – all things to look forward to. But do try my other recipes based on the normally available produce because you can, usually, find similar ingredients in your own locality.

Watercress and Comté Cheese Omelette

Watercress is a robust green vegetable. Those bags of limp, tasteless greens that you can buy in the supermarket are not at all what I have in mind here. It's just not worth the bother of making even these simple dishes if that's all you can get hold of. Wait until watercress is in season and buy, if you are able, locally grown bunches of fresh crunchy stalks and peppery dark green leaves. If you've gathered the watercress yourself make sure the water in which it is growing is pollution free, and when you get it home wash it really well in plenty of cold running water. Wrap in a clean tea towel and pat dry.

For this recipe chop the watercress rather coarsely, using a good proportion of stalks to leaves.

It is hard to produce more than one omelette at a time and once cooked it needs to be slid immediately onto a hot plate and eaten straight away. I think of this as a simple lunchtime meal for two – one being the cook. So lay the table beforehand, heat up the plates and don't stand on ceremony, cook and serve his/hers, then make yours.

For a successful omelette, ideally, you need to use a heavy based, but not too big, non-stick pan.

Allow 3 eggs per person

For two omelettes
    50 grams mature Comté cheese, grated
    2 good handfuls of watercress, roughly chopped
    3 tablespoons thick cream or crème fraîche
    Maldon sea salt and freshly ground pepper
    a dash of Tabasco
    6 eggs
    1 tablespoon water
    10-20g butter

Mix the grated cheese, watercress, cream, a little salt and pepper and a dash of Tabasco together in a bowl and leave to one side.

Break the eggs into a bowl, add a dessertspoon of water, season with salt and pepper, and beat briskly with a fork. Heat the frying pan and once hot, quickly swirl in a little butter (ideally clarified so that you can cook at a high temperature without the butter burning) around to coat the inside of the pan. Pour in the beaten eggs and cook for 15-20 seconds just so they begin to lightly set on the bottom. Using the side of a fork scrape the sides to the middle. Carry on stirring and gently shaking the pan. Once the egg is set but still slightly runny, spoon half of the cheese and watercress mix down the centre of the omelette. Allow 30 seconds or so for it to heat through, then with the help of a fork, flip half the omelette over towards the middle while tilting the pan, roll the omelette completely over onto itself and slide onto a heated plate. Make an incision with a knife down the length of the omelette to expose a little of the filling, then brush the top of the omelette with melted butter.

Serve immediately on a heated plate

Watercress and Lettuce Soup

The French often use lettuce as a vegetable. I think because they are fundamentally quite frugal and nothing gets wasted, not even the bolting lettuces. At the same time their long tradition of cooking and eating well means that they have the skills to turn even a few left-overs, some vegetable peelings or the bones of fish and fowl into quite delicious bowls of food. This soup, found in the pages of Amanda Hesser's great book *The Cook and the Gardener*, is just such a one.

For four
2 tablespoons olive oil
2 shallots, finely chopped
3 good handfuls watercress, thick stems removed and leaves well washed
1 lettuce trimmed and washed (almost any type will do but the soft butterhead
*   lettuce is best)*

850 ml chicken or vegetable stock
150 ml milk
2 tablespoons double cream or crème fraîche
Maldon sea salt and freshly ground black pepper

In a large saucepan gently heat the olive oil. Add the shallot and cook until soft and translucent – about 3 to 4 minutes. Add the watercress and lettuce by the handful, stirring them around for a couple of minutes, so that they wilt in the heat. Add the stock. Bring to the boil, then turn the heat down to a gentle simmer for just another 2 or 3 minutes.

Allow the soup to cool a little and then ladle it into a blender. You may need to do this in two goes. Process the soup until it is smooth with just small flecks of green. It should be quite thick. Return to the pan.

Add the milk and cream and reheat but do not allow to boil. Taste and add seasoning.

As Amanda says, for such a simple and quickly made soup the taste return is enormous. Serve it warm with a few fried croutons. It is a lovely starter to serve before a spring meal of lamb or chicken.

Gratin of Chicory with Ham in a Cheese Sauce

They call it endive and we call it chicory – or is it the other way round? Whatever – we are talking about those blanched buds of leaves, tightly furled, white with a touch of yellow at their edges. In the UK they are most likely to be consigned to the salad bowl. The crisp leaves do work well in salads but, even better, they make a superb cooked vegetable, especially in the winter when there's not much else around.

How prosaic this dish sounds and it is indeed very easy to make. Yet every person I have ever served it to, even those who profess to disliking chicory, gobbles it up and comes back for more.

What's the secret? This is a vegetable that needs long slow cooking to really come into its own. The slight bitterness softens but does not quite disappear. Balance that bitter edge with some sweetness and a little salt and chicory is truly delicious. Cook them as in the recipe below in honey and butter to a state of delectable caramelisation and serve as a side dish to baked gammon. Otherwise wrap each chicory bulb in a thick piece of country ham lightly spread with grain mustard, and finish in a sauce made with mature Comté cheese.

This is a comforting winter lunch or supper dish and is easy to make well in advance if friends are eating with you. I usually serve it with a dish of slow roasted tomatoes.

And plenty of bread.

For four
> *allow 2 chicory bulbs per person, or, if they are very big, slice in two*
> > *longitudinally and serve two halves per person*
> *Maldon sea salt*
> *60g butter*
> *1-2 tablespoons light flavoured runny honey (Acacia is good)*
> *8 slices of boiled country ham*
> *grain mustard to spread on the ham*

For the cheese sauce
> *20g butter*
> *15g plain flour*
> *140ml milk*
> *140ml single cream, or use all milk*
> *½ teaspoon Dijon mustard*

50g Comté cheese, grated

50g Parmesan, grated

Malden sea salt and freshly ground black pepper

nutmeg

squeeze of lemon

The trick with chicory is to cook it long and slow.

First, with a sharp knife cut out a little cone from the central core at the base of each chicory. One is always advised to do this though I'm not sure exactly why except that I assume a) it removes some of the bitterness and b) aids the cooking process.

Place the chicory in a pan – I prefer to use a large shallow-sided pan with a see-through lid. This way I can have just one layer of chicory and see what's going on. Pour on boiling water to just cover the chicory and add a generous pinch or two of sea salt. Bring to the boil, put the lid on, then turn the heat down so that the contents are quietly simmering. After about twenty minutes, test the doneness of the chicory by checking with a sharp knife at the point where the chicory bulb is most dense. If there is any resistance continue cooking a little longer – for about another ten minutes or until the centre feels soft.

Drain in a colander, leaving the chicory pointing downwards. Allow it to cool so that you can gently squeeze out any residual water from the leaves.

Wash and dry the pan and add the butter. Heat it through to melt then put the chicory back in one layer. Turn them well in the butter. Drizzle the honey over the chicory, add a pinch of sea salt and cover with the lid. Allow to continue cooking on a low heat for another 20 minutes. Turn them occasionally. The chicory will exude more water. Remove the lid, turn up the heat and cook off the residual water, keeping a sharp eye on the pan. Once the water has gone you will be left with the butter and honey, which will begin to coat the chicory. Keep turning the chicory until all the outer leaves are a rich golden colour. Do not allow them to burn.

Return the finished chicory to the colander and once again let it drain pointing it downwards. Leave until it is cool enough to handle. Squeeze the chicory gently to remove any residual water.

Spread each slice of ham with a smear of grain mustard. Lay one chicory (or a half if they are very big) on the slice of ham and roll it up. Repeat until each chicory is wrapped in its slice of ham.

Place them to fit snugly together in a well buttered ovenproof dish. Leave to one side while you make the cheese sauce.

In a saucepan melt the butter. Remove from the heat and add the flour. Mix it well making sure there are no lumps. Add a little of the milk to make a thin looking sauce. Place the pan on a low heat, add the rest of the milk and cream and the Dijon mustard, stirring briskly all the time. Keep stirring the sauce over a gentle heat until it begins to thicken and comes to the boil. Keeping the heat low so the sauce is just plopping away gently. Stir occasionally and cook for at least 10 minutes. This is to ensure that the flour is properly cooked.

Remove from heat and beat in both the cheeses. Taste and add salt if required, a grinding of pepper and a few shavings of nutmeg. Pour the sauce over the ham wrapped chicory. Top with a few dabs of butter and place in an preheated oven 200C/Gas 6 for about 20 minutes. To brown the top, sprinkle the gratin with more grated cheese – a mix of both – and place under the grill.

Sweetbreads with Morels in a Creamy Sauce

The people of Cambrai adore their *abats* and of all the innard-y bits and pieces subsumed under this French word for offal surely it is sweetbreads that would beguile and convert the most suspicious of eaters. They are as dainty and delicious as their name implies. This recipe from Simon Hopkinson's *Roast Chicken and Other Stories* is much simpler than most of the French recipes I have tried when making this dish. I think it's the best one.

For four
> *25-30 dried morels**
> *75g butter*
> *2 carrots, peeled and chopped small*
> *1 stick celery, chopped small*
> *1 leek, cleaned and finely sliced*
> *2 medium tomatoes, chopped*
> *Maldon sea salt and freshly ground black pepper*
> *½ bottle dry white wine*
> *500g calves sweetbreads (preferably heartbreads or 'noix')*

For the sauce
> *50g butter*
> *2 shallots, peeled and finely chopped*
> *1 small wine glass of dry Madeira*
> *425ml whipping cream (if in France use bottled crème fluide or fleurette)*
> *juice ½ lemon*
> *1 tablespoon fresh chives, chopped*

First, soak the morels in about 600ml of warm water for at least 30 minutes.

In a wide, shallow-sided pan with a lid, melt the butter and gently cook the vegetables until a pale golden colour. Season and add the wine. Bring to the boil then turn down to a mere simmer.

Put the sweetbreads in the pan of vegetables in a single layer and braise them over a gentle heat for a couple of minutes, turning them from time to time. Cover and continue to cook over a very gentle heat for about 10 more minutes. Avoid over-cooking, prodding them gently with the tip of a sharp knife to check they're not hardening. Once cooked, lift them out of the braising liquid, removing any vegetables adhering to them and place them on a flat plate. Cover with another plate weighted down with a couple of tins of something – your choice. The sweetbreads need to be pressed fairly flat and left to cool. Once cold they are much easier to prepare.

Meanwhile strain the vegetables, reserving the liquid. Strain the morel soaking water through a very fine sieve (or wet muslin) into the vegetable liquid, giving the morels a good squeeze and set them to one side. Bring the liquid to a boil and reduce by about three-quarters.

Once the sweetbreads are cold peel off the thin membrane that surrounds each one with a sharp knife, also removing any bits of gristle and fat.

Cut into small slices and reserve.

Make the sauce: pour the reduced vegetable stock into a container and leave to one side. Clean the pan and in it melt the 50g of butter. Add the shallots and fry to a pale gold. Now add the morels and very gently sauté for five minutes or so. Pour in the Madeira and reduce until almost gone. Add the vegetable stock. Stir and cook to a syrupy consistency. Check for seasoning.

Add the cream.

Add the sweetbreads and bring pan to a gentle simmer. Cook until the sauce is the thickness of thin custard. Add the lemon juice and chives and check the seasoning.

I like to serve this with fresh tagliatelle.

Serve on heated plates with a scattering of chopped chives to finish.

(*See My Store Cupboard Favourites, p.238)

Flemish Beef Carbonnade with Pain d'Épices

This dish is very much of the north where grapes do not grow, instead beer is the tipple of choice and often used in cooking. However, too much beer in a stew can be a little overpowering and can make it taste bitter. Part beer and part stock helps to overcome this, as does long slow cooking. This casserole is a great dish for an informal supper with friends in the depths of winter and is especially good if cooked the day before. Reheat and finish with the pain d'épices (a type of gingerbread) when you intend to serve it. The addition of the ginger bread (you can use ordinary bread if you can't get it) gives the *carbonnade* an authentic Flemish touch.

For four

> oil (or better still beef dripping)
> 1 kg beef shin, cut into good sized chunks
> 4 medium onions, peeled and each one sliced downwards into about 6 segments
> 250g of chestnut mushrooms, cleaned and trimmed as necessary
> bouquet garni (bay, garlic, parsley, thyme all tied up in half a celery stalk)
> Maldon sea salt and freshly ground black pepper
> 450ml brown beer
> 300ml beef stock (I often use Knorr concentrated beef stock*)
> about a dessertspoon of soft brown sugar
> grated nutmeg
> 1-2 teaspoons aged balsamic vinegar or Worcester sauce
> several slices of pain d'épices – enough to create a thin layer on the top of the
>   casserole
> 1 dessertspoon Dijon mustard

Over a medium heat in a cast iron casserole, warm the oil or melt the dripping. Then brown the beef on all sides. Lift out and put to one side. Throw in the onions and fry briskly, adding a little more oil if necessary. After a few minutes add the mushrooms. Lower the heat and leave to colour for 10 minutes. Replace the beef and add the bouquet garni and a little salt. Pour in the beer and stock to cover the beef. Bring to a gentle simmer on the top of the stove and remove any scum that rises to the top.

Place in the oven and cook for between 2½ - 3 hours at 160C/Gas 3 until the meat is cooked and the beer has lost its bitterness. Season with salt, pepper, brown sugar, nutmeg and a little balsamic vinegar or Worcester sauce. As always do this little by little. My measures for seasoning are just a guide. Keep tasting and use your own judgement.

About 40 minutes before serving, remove the bouquet garni and skim off any fat. Raise the oven temperature to 200C/Gas 6. Spread the slices of pain d'épices with mustard and arrange on top of the casserole, mustard side down. Push the bread down below the surface so that it is well soaked in gravy. It will rise back up to the top. Leave off the lid, return to the oven and cook for another 30-40 minutes until the pain d'épices is looking crisp.

I would serve this with a buttery mash of celeriac and potato.

(*See My Store Cupboard Favourites, p.234)

Crème Brûlée à la Chicorée

Who doesn't like crème brûlée? It's my favourite dessert when in France and always on the menu in the excellent family run restaurant close by the basin in Cambrai where we moor our boat.

In the Nord/Pas de Calais regions the people there still have a taste for the wartime coffee substitute made from ground chicory root. If you are unable to track down a bottle of liquid chicory essence (easily found in most French supermarkets) then use Camp coffee instead.

For four
> *200ml full-fat milk*
> *200ml double cream or thick crème fraîche*
> *4 large egg yolks*
> *40g sugar*
> *1 tablespoon plus 2 teaspoons of liquid chicory essence or Camp coffee*
> *Demerara sugar, to cover*

Preheat the oven to 150C/Gas 2.

Heat the milk and cream together to just below boiling point. Lightly beat the egg yolks with the sugar and pour the hot milk and cream over them, beating the mixture well as you do it. Stir in the coffee/chicory essence and pour through a sieve into a jug.

Divide the mixture between four 85 mm ramekins.

Place them in a roasting tin or similar and put the tin in the oven. Pour boiling water into the tin, allowing it to come about two thirds of the way up the sides of the ramekins.

Bake for about 30 minutes, until they are set but still wobbly in the middle. Remove and leave to cool, then cover with clingfilm and chill in the fridge for at least three hours. They can be made up to two days ahead and kept in the fridge.

To serve – sprinkle with the Demerara sugar and either use a blow torch to glaze the surface or place them under a very hot grill until the sugar has melted. They can be prepared up to two hours before serving.

CHAPTER 2

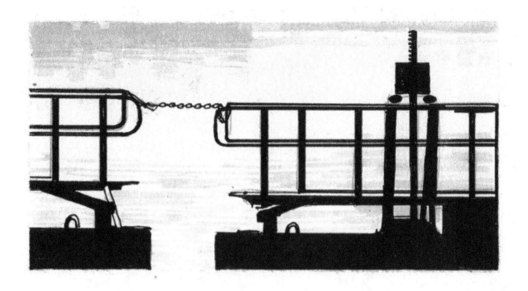

On Our Way at Last

We leave Cambrai in early June, towards the end of the asparagus season. Before leaving I go to Mr Gosselet's, just across the canal from where we are moored, to get the last really fresh fruit and veg we'll be able to buy for a while. It is a long established market garden where the whole Gosselet tribe of several generations all seem to be employed and, happily, appear to be making a very good living.

At this time of year the little shop is a veritable Aladdin's cave stuffed full of the freshest of salads, vegetables and summer fruits. Here I can buy my favourite potatoes, as well as small, delicately flavoured, purple-skinned turnips, freshly cut frisée lettuce, and properly peppery radishes. The shop, part of an old farm outbuilding, is cool and dark; there's a small, rather cobwebby window, with the only other light coming in at the door when it is open and not crowded with eager shoppers. So full of produce, there is barely space for the customers; we must queue outside. It's a bit like queuing for the ladies loo – you wait until someone comes out then it's your turn to go in. Make no mistake though, this is a very special queue and certainly not one to get cross about having to stand in; it is part of the Gosselet experience and it is in this queue that I have learned some of my most useful French and been the recipient of any number of recipes, including several variations of same. Mr Gosselet's customers tend to be a noisy lot, particularly the pensioners, who in response to my timid enquiries, start to argue amongst themselves as to the correct way to cook this fruit or that veg. My best words learned so far are *'une poignée'*, which correctly translated means 'wrist' but also means, more loosely, 'a handful'. Surely this is the most important of all measures in the world of greengrocery? It's not a word I would ever have thought to use had it not been for my helpful teachers here in the queue. Now I can ask for 'a small handful of green beans, please', 'a big handful of those girolle mushrooms', 'just a handful or two of these cherries', all in my best French, knowing that I will be served exactly the amount I am after without having to recall what, say, 500 grams of stuff looks like.

I buy *'une grosse poignée'* of the very last of Mr G's white asparagus even though for the past few weeks we have rather overdosed on the stuff. It is a major crop up here in northern France and really cheap to buy in season. The fat stems look so fresh and tender I just can't resist. I have been experimenting with various ways of cooking and serving them and at this price the odd disaster won't bankrupt us. In any case, there will be no more now until next year.

In amongst his bunches of fresh herbs I spot purslane – one of my favourite 'light' greens which along with spinach, rocket and sorrel, is a tasty addition to soups and salads. Purslane is also delicious served as a vegetable lightly turned in butter and eaten warm. Often regarded as nothing more than a nuisance weed, in the wild it tends to be a ground coverer and is therefore quite small. Mr Gosselet grows a garden variety that is an altogether bigger beast. So I'll take a couple of bunches please, and some tiny Charlottes, a big bag of peas in their pods, radishes and ten eggs (with apologies for not bringing something to put them in). As usual, and after the fact, I realise I have bought far too much by way of courgettes, peppers, fennel and new red onions, so will spend a little time once we were on the move, making *the* ratatouille. It's a useful standby especially when we are traveling; it will keep in the fridge for a few days and works just as well eaten cold as hot.

With the bit still firmly between teeth I point to a wooden punnet of deeply crimson strawberries, load up with mint, parsley and some tarragon for the chicken, put half a dozen new garlic bulbs into my basket and choose a great big bunch of Sweet William – the only flowers that Mr Gosselet allows to grow amongst his rows of vegetables. That about completes my purchases and I happily stagger off with it all back to the boat.

Earlier I had bought a shoulder of lamb from the butcher's and a free range chicken in the market; unpasteurised milk, crème fraîche, some aged Comté cheese and a Tarte Maroilles from the dairy farmer's stall; good keeping bread and a brioche loaf from the baker. I reckoned we were about ready to go with no need to stop for provisions for quite some time.

The St Quentin Canal is a favourite waterway. It is part of our home territory, a canal upon which we travel frequently, to and from Cambrai in the Nord-Pas de Calais region, where we sometimes leave *Friesland* during the winter. Virtually no pleasure boats are to be found on it, other than one or two en route to warmer climes, this being far too northerly for our sun-seeking brethren to want to hang about in for long.

There is still enough commercial traffic – family run barges which carry about 350 tons of freight and are around 39 metres long – to keep us on our toes but usually we have the canal to ourselves; almost our only human contact nowadays is the occasional itinerant lock-keeper. He turns up when a lock's automatic mechanism suffers some small failure, then we can exchange a few words. Although there are plenty of villages on this and most of the other canals we will be using on our way to Strasbourg, few have shops any more. Much of the barge trade, once the mainstay of a busy working waterway, has long since slipped away and with it the canal-side bars, the bakers, the grocers and general stores, and, saddest of all for us, practically all the simple restaurants that once served the working boat community.

In the past, the boatmen and their families, who all lived on board, were concerned, like us, to have a loaf on the table most days. No supermarkets on every corner then nor large freezers tucked away somewhere on board for them, or indeed for us either, but usually a small canal-side shop a step away from the lock would have, along with other provisions, some bread for sale. During the long days of boating one needs something that sustains; a simple meal that can be quickly thrown together and is easy to eat on the move. A baguette, stuffed with a few salad leaves, a slice of ham or cheese, will keep us going until we tie up for the night. So we take our cue from the traveling people, which means being ever alert to the signs that there is bread to be had nearby.

After the Revolution, Napoleon cannily decreed that all citizens must have a daily supply of good fresh bread and that the price be fixed by law. At the time, much of the anger and frustration, which ultimately led to the population revolting, had more to do with the price and quality of bread than any deep-seated desire to overthrow the aristocracy and clergy. However, once seen to be a successful ruse, it's all too easy to make a habit of revolution; how best to keep the peasants calm and reasonably content would have been a major preoccupation of the governing classes at the time. A cheap and constant supply of daily bread was the obvious answer. Thus, as a result of Boney's decree, even today, when there is no longer a resident baker in the village, there still has to be a *dépôt de pain* – that is somewhere bread is delivered to each day where the locals can buy it. More usually nowadays, a bread van arrives at a designated time and stops in the village centre; a blast on its horn brings everyone running. For boats passing through on the canal it is just chance if you spot the van and lucky circumstance if you happen to be in a lock or close to a bridge at the time and can persuade the driver to hurl a baguette your way. So on a longish journey with few towns to stop at en route we take really good keeping bread with us; carefully wrapped and contained it will stay fresh for a few days and be fine thereafter for toast; ultimately if there is any left it gets turned into croutons, crispbread and finally breadcrumbs. When it runs out and the bread van proves elusive – I make some. To make 'proper' bread you really need to be moored up for a few hours. When we are on the move my job as 'the crew' means I must be ever alert to the needs of the boating – ready to steer if necessary and always available to work locks. Bread making requires calm and steadiness. Instead, for a quick fix, you can't beat an Irish soda loaf. It doesn't keep for long but is speedily made, requires no yeast and is quite delicious.

The St Quentin canal is famous for having the longest tunnel in France, just under six kilometres. I like the tunnel and to be towed through it is to become part of French canal history. Once, all craft were towed everywhere on French waterways, either by men or horses and even donkeys and in later times by some form of traction engine which ran along the towpath. Until the 1980s, working barges, although long since motorised, were still obliged to be towed across the whole of the St Quentin summit pound which includes two tunnels. Now we are allowed to cross it under our own power with the sole exception of the longer of the two tunnels – the Riqueval. Through this we must still be towed.

There is something about a tunnel that always makes me want to boil up bones. Don't know why, though there's not a lot else to do in one. I find myself thinking I'll just make some stock with the last of that chicken carcass. A few minutes later the idea is sharply knocked on the head. As my saucepan full of bits and bones comes to the boil, Captain shouts down from the wheelhouse above that the windows are all steaming up and he can't see a bloody thing through them. This is not good at a time where a certain amount of vigilance is called for; when one's Captain is trying to keep his barge on course, stopping it from hitting the rocky tunnel walls and without an engine to assist. I rapidly turn off the gas.

Instead I put the lamb into the oven, having first sat the joint on a thick bed of well oiled onions, lightly salted and sugared, scattered with sprigs of fresh rosemary and a handful of unpeeled new garlic cloves. The onions will slowly break down and brown over the next few hours. Every so often when I check on how the meat is doing I add a slosh of vermouth to the meat tin.

The world divides into those who like their food wet and those who prefer it dry. We are part of the wet lot, so gravy, sauces and dressings are essential to our enjoyment of food. I do like a big jug of gravy with a roast. Later, when the lamb is cooked and resting, I'll add water and a little more wine to what has become a richly caramelised oniony residue and reduce it down to a gravy to die for. I will steam some of Mr Gosselet's tiny potatoes in their skins. Once cooked and drained they can be left on a very low heat, in a covered saucepan with a drop of water, a dollop of butter and a pinch of salt. As the water reduces almost to nothing the potatoes slowly turn brown in the butter. You need to keep an eye on them though as they can burn, but usually they will sit quite happily at the back of the stove on a very low gas. I'll give the saucepan the odd shake or two while I make the gravy and argue myself into cooking some wholly unnecessary green beans. It's just to add colour to the plate really. Captain, old-fashioned fellow that he is, still likes his roast lamb served up with a bit of mint sauce; this is much more palatable made with some sweet balsamic and a little mild honey, rather than the sharp vinegar and sugar mix our mums used to go in for, so I mix that up too.

The joint is on the large side but cooked lamb reheats well and is perfect boating food; there will be enough for several more meals. Sooner or later all the old standbys will make it to the table: shepherd's pie, hotpot, spag bol, curry or something tagine-y – even good old-fashioned rissoles. Lamb and ratatouille make perfect partners so dinners for the next few days will be a doddle. In the meantime we still have a long day ahead of us.

When we finally emerge into the daylight nearly two hours later the tug pulls over, the barges we have been following start their engines, drop off their towlines and, as they are all empty, begin to pull quickly away from us. Standing on the fore-end of *Friesland* I wait for the last barge to throw off our line and I heave it in; it is wet, heavy, and covered in green weed. Hidden from view in the deep cutting, we motor steadily across the narrow summit pound, until finally emerging into the sunlight and a more open landscape. Then on to the outskirts of St Quentin itself where we begin the steady lock by lock drop down towards the Aisne valley.

After so many months of being moored up in a town, we all, *Friesland* too I feel, are quickly finding our way back into our natural environment. A quiet content settles; we are absorbed in our activity; we smile that conspiratorial smile at each other and begin to relax, falling into the rhythm of the boating – a slow and steady beat provided by *Friesland's* classic Gardner engine.

The locks supply the counterpoint, coming as they do, at regular intervals. We have a system for working through them so well assimilated that it requires no discussion. On this particular waterway the locks work automatically. As we approach, Captain waves our 'zapper' in its direction and the lock readies itself for us; we slowly creep ever closer. As the gates open, he steers *Friesland* rapidly into the chamber. From my usual station on the fore-end I chuck a rope over a bollard set close to the edge of the lock, then take a turn or two around the boat's own double bitts which act as a brake, bringing *Friesland* to a gentle halt. Captain holds her steady in forward gear while I operate the 'tirette', which sets off the next stage of the locking process: the gates close behind us and the water begins to empty out of the chamber. We drop gently down in the cool damp-walled lock, wait for the water inside and out to make a level and then, as the gates open, I flick the rope off the bollard, which is now way above my head, coiling it back down onto the deck where it lives. These actions, repeated a thousand times, are as familiar to us as breathing and almost as unconscious. This is our sort of boating, our real life, and it feels good to be doing it again.

RECIPES

The secret of good cooking lies first in the quality of the ingredients and then in timing and temperature. Some things are easier to cook than others. Easy is good when one is boating. None of the recipes below need to be too finely judged. Trust your palate and your instincts. Add herbs and spices incrementally, tasting as you go – you can always add a little more of something but too much tipped in all at once can't be removed and you may have just ruined your dinner.

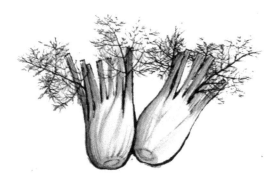

Ratatouille

I walked down into the lock-keeper's garden. He waved his hand around – take whatever you want the gesture implied. We picked red and green peppers, both mild and spicy, yellow courgettes and purple aubergines. Huge ripe tomatoes were hanging from vines and long pink shallots were bunched and hooked onto his fence to dry. He loaded them into my basket and heaped a dozen small fennel bulbs on top. I begged him to stop. But, he says, you must have some garlic and parsley as well. How, otherwise, could I ever hope to cook a proper ratatouille? 'How much for the lot then?' 'Three euros', he says, 'Here, have these green tomatoes as well, a little *cadeau*, in case you want to make a *confiture*.'

My own ratatouille has slowly evolved. Over the years there have been a few changes. Nowadays I prefer to leave out the aubergines. They tend to soak up oil and their texture in this dish never seems quite right to me. I often use fennel instead. I also like to spice my ratatouille up a bit with ground cumin, sweet smoky paprika and a little chilli. I have found too that I prefer the texture of vegetables that have been slow roasted rather than when they have been cooked on the stovetop in a pan. This last discovery came about as a direct result of cooking while on the move: heavily locked sections of canal preclude spending too much time stirring pots and checking on the food. Long slow cooking in an oven reduces liquid content slowly, which means the ingredients stay firmer and introduces the process of caramelisation – both of which greatly improve the taste. The vegetables retain their colour too. Using the oven for cooking, especially when there are a lot of locks to take care of means I am free to help out as crew when the need arises.

Ratatouille 1: On Top of the Stove Version

The thing about ratatouille is that each vegetable should shine individually but at the same time the finished dish needs to be a rich amalgam of everything in the pot. Essentially this means adding each one in turn, depending on how long it takes to cook, using plenty of olive oil, and making sure that there is very little liquid. Nothing should be cooked to a mush. For me the end product must be an amalgam of the vivid colours and the distinctive flavours of each of the ingredients used. And it's always better eaten the following day.

For four people with some left over
  2-3 red onions, halved and cut downwards to make chunky slivers
  olive oil
  2 crushed (with the flat of a knife) cloves of garlic
  2 red peppers - centres removed, the skins cut into wide strips

1-2 mild fresh green chillies – inside pith and seeds removed, then finely sliced

2 heads of Italian fennel – outer leaves removed, then sliced downwards into 6-8 sections

3-4 small courgettes cut into chunky slices (yellow ones – for their colour, but green will do)

a teaspoon of dried oregano

4 good-sized ripe, skinned, de-pipped tomatoes – the big droopy Italian ones, French Cœur de Bœuf or Andine Cornue are best. They tend to have a greater proportion of flesh to juice, giving plenty of rich flavour without too much liquid.

Maldon sea salt and freshly ground black pepper

a few drops of aged balsamic vinegar

Parsley or fresh oregano

Give the sliced onions a head start of about ten minutes, cooking them gently in olive oil without letting them colour, then add the crushed garlic, the sliced peppers and the sliced chillies. Another ten minutes or so and you can throw in the fennel followed by the courgettes. Make sure everything gets a good coating of olive oil and leave to cook gently together in the pan with the lid on over a low heat for 10 minutes.

Add a generous teaspoonful of dried oregano and mix it in.

Finally, add the skinned tomatoes from which you have squeezed out the juice and pips and roughly chopped. Gently fold everything together.

Cook everything at a gentle simmer in a nice big Le Creuset casserole dish (or other heavy pot which will distribute the heat evenly). This will take around 45 minutes. Check occasionally to see how it is doing. If there is a lot of liquid leave the lid off to reduce it. If the vegetables are cooked sufficiently, pour off the excess liquid and reduce it down in another pan, then pour it back into the finished ratatouille. Do keep checking as there are any number of variables which can alter the cooking time. (By this I mean the quality and age of the vegetables, the pot you are cooking it in, as well as the controllability of the heat being applied, and indeed the cooking medium itself.) You should end up with a lovely unctuous mess of vegetables, soft but not disintegrating. The tomato will have reduced to a thick sauce. Now you can taste and add salt and pepper, maybe a little sugar. Finally, if you like, add a few drops of aged balsamic vinegar.

Finish with a splash more of olive oil and strew with plenty of fresh chopped parsley or, as it grows so profusely along the towpath, some sprigs of fresh oregano.

Eat it warm, ideally, with little pink lamb chops and plenty of crusty bread or have it cold with cheese and cooked meats or with whatever else you fancy will go with it. Even eat it on its own, straight out of the fridge, in the middle of the night. Like most casserole-ey things this improves greatly if made the day before; it then just needs a gentle reheat.

Ratatouille 2: The Roasted Version

Preheat the oven to 180C/Gas 5

Use all the ingredients listed above but replace the fresh green chilli with a goodly pinch of dried red. Cut all the vegetables into similar-sized pieces and stir them together in a bowl. Leave out the dried oregano and instead add a teaspoon of powdered cumin, a teaspoon of fennel seeds and a teaspoon sweet smoky paprika, plus plenty of salt and pepper and a good slug of olive oil. Gently mix all the vegetables and spices together with your hands to ensure that all are covered with a good coating of oil. Tip everything into a large open meat tray, or similar, and roast in the centre of the oven for about 45-60 minutes. (I also like to add several unpeeled garlic cloves to cook in one corner of the roasting tray. I fish them out at the end of the cooking time, peel and squeeze out the lovely soft garlic paste, mixing it back into the finished ratatouille.) Check on how the vegetables are doing a couple of times, stirring them around occasionally to prevent them sticking. If need be, turn up the oven a little towards the end of the cooking time, so that they begin to caramelise here and there. Once everything is cooked, remove the tray from the oven, mash down the tomatoes a little, squeeze out the now soft garlic and mix into the roasted veg. Add a splash of water – just enough to bring a little moisture to the mix. Stir everything together gently, check the seasoning and serve warm.

Things To Do with Leftover Ratatouille

- Spice it up with some chopped subrosada and/or chorizo sausage and to make a complete meal, add a tin of haricot or butter beans.

- In a wide shallow pan fry some chopped chorizo, add the ratatouille and if it is very solid, a little water. Bring to a simmer, then making indentations with a serving spoon, break an egg into each one and cook gently until the white is set but the yolk is still runny. It helps the cooking of the eggs if, at this point, you cover the pan with a lid for a couple of minutes.

- Add more ground cumin, fennel and pimento and a little bit of chilli (check the seasoning all the time as it will already be fairly spicy). Cook gently for a few minutes then add a tin of chickpeas (remove the skins by emptying the chickpeas into a bowl and filling the bowl with cold water. Rub the peas with your hands and the skins will come off easily). If the consistency of the ratatouille is very thick, add some water. Eat it with merguez sausages or a lamb brochette, or both, or just with couscous for a veggie option. Provide additional heat with a spoonful of harissa paste.

- Process left-over ratatouille to a sauce-like consistency. Heat it gently. Eat it as is or add a little crème fraîche to mellow the flavour. Mix with tagliatelle or gnocchi and finish with flakes of Parmesan.

Chargrilled Asparagus with a Fig Balsamic Dressing and Slivers of Aged Parmesan

I think this tastes and looks more appealing when made with green asparagus, but really either green or white will do. It's an excellent starter especially if you are planning a meal with an Italian feel. I would probably allow about half a dozen stalks per person, depending upon their size (the asparagus, not the people), and put it before a pasta dish such as Sweetbreads with Morels in a Creamy Sauce (see p.32), finishing the meal with Champagne and Elderflower Jelly (see p.153). The original recipe comes from *Sally Clarke's Book*, published in 1999 but now, I suspect, out of print.

The asparagus should be fresh and crisp. There is rarely any need to peel the the stems of the green but if using white, which often have fatter stems than the green, I peel them using a horizontal potato peeler. Then I snap off the ends at their natural breaking point; this ensures that there are no fibrous chewy bits to spoil the meal.

The asparagus, if green, needs only a minute or two to cook in boiling salted water; drain it and cool it rapidly in cold water while it is still quite crisp. White takes a bit longer to cook. Whichever type you are cooking keep an eye on them as you will be chargrilling the stems to finish, so at this stage they need to be slightly undercooked. Test with the sharp point of a knife. Dry the asparagus, pour over a little olive oil and a sprinkling of Maldon sea salt, using your hands to make sure all the stalks are lightly coated. Leave to one side until ready to finish.

You can, if you wish, and the asparagus stems are very slender, leave out the cooking in water stage and simply chargrill them just before serving. I tend to parboil because it produces a more reliable texture, and removes the hassle of everything needing to be done at once and at the last minute.

Shave off flakes of Parmesan from a lump of well aged cheese.

When ready to serve, heat up a ridged pan until very hot indeed and lay the oil-coated asparagus across the ridges. Cook and turn just long enough for the asparagus to acquire nice dark stripes on each side.

Fan out the asparagus across large heated plates. Drizzle over the figgy balsamic, lightly shower the plate with some really grassy tasting olive oil and finish with the Parmesan flakes. A slice or two of good ciabatta will definitely be needed to mop up the juices.

Fig Balsamic Dressing

some really good aged balsamic vinegar
a few dried figs softened in hot water and finely chopped
    or a little savoury fig relish (shop bought is fine), well chopped
a little water
extra virgin olive oil
a few drops of lemon juice

Simply mix these ingredients together. The amount you need depends on how many you are feeding. Start with a dessertspoon of balsamic and about the same of well-chopped dried figs or relish. A good quality fig-flavoured balsamic mixed with a drizzle of honey is also a good replacement if you have no fig relish. Taste while you make it. Thin down with a little water if necessary and sharpen up with a few drops of lemon juice. Beat some olive oil into the dressing – this will give it more body. Keep mixing and tasting until you have sufficient to do a really good drizzle over each serving. Supply bread. You will find people like to wipe their plates clean.

Three Purslane Recipes

Purslane, along with sorrel, rocket and wild asparagus, is one of my most favourite summer greens; I look forward to gathering it in the wild or buying some along with all my other bunches of herbs in the market. In the distant past it was popular in both Italy and England. Today though, it is hardly known or used in the UK, although there is absolutely no reason not to grow it as a salad vegetable in the garden or allotment. It is easy to grow. Just keep cutting and it will keep coming; if you don't want it to spread everywhere don't let it go to seed.

Anna Del Conte, who obviously shares my mission to make it better known, tells us in her book *Amaretto, Apple Cake and Artichokes* that she gets her seeds from Jekka's Herb Farm in the UK. She also says that you can sometimes buy bunches of it fresh from Greek and Chinese shops in London and other big cities. The Chinese call it 'yin choy'.

In France it is called *pourpier* and can usually be bought, found or grown in most parts from June onwards. The leaves are very succulent with a slightly astringent flavour. If you have plenty, blanch it quickly in boiling water, drain, then cook gently in butter for a minute or so, season and serve as a vegetable like samphire. If you only have a few leaves, add them raw to a green salad to give it a little acidic bite.

Below are three recipes to get you started. The original of the first one is found in *La Cuisine de Madame Saint-Ange*, a book published by Larousse in 1927 and reprinted in 1958. The cooking time was very long; perhaps garden peas were larger and tougher then. My version here has a lightly sharp tang to it, the peas are soft and though the colour, due to the sludgy hue of sorrel, is not beautiful, it does taste very good.

Purslane, Sorrel and Green Pea Soup

For two or three
>   *30g purslane leaves*
>   *60g sorrel*
>   *½ teaspoon dill*
>   *40g chopped young white (or spring) onions, chopped*
>   *60g unsalted butter*
>   *500ml hot water or light stock*
>   *500g fresh shelled or frozen peas*
>   *Maldon sea salt to taste*
>   *Freshly ground white pepper*

Chop the purslane leaves very finely. Remove any large stalks from the sorrel and chop that finely too. Chop the dill. Put the onion in a heavy non-stick pan with half of the butter. Place over low heat and stew gently for about 10 minutes; add the purslane and sorrel and cook all together for a further 10 minutes. Stir occasionally with a wooden spoon. Let nothing stick or brown.

Add the hot water or stock. Bring to the boil, add the peas and turn heat down to a gentle simmer for a further 20 minutes. At the end of the cooking time remove from heat. When cool purée two thirds of the soup. Remix with the remaining soup, gently reheating and adding the rest of the butter. Taste and season with salt and pepper. Resist adding a swirl of cream as the sorrel tends to cause it to curdle slightly.

Fattoush

This is a Middle Eastern salad which I think most people will be familiar with. We eat it (or approximations of it) frequently. It's particularly good during the summer when everything has that fresh, just out of the ground, intensity of flavour.

An essential ingredient of this salad, purslane, is one which I was rarely able to obtain before we came to France. Here, at certain times of the year it is a rampant weed. To be rid of it, I just pull it up and eat it; would that bindweed were so easy to deal with.

This recipe is the one I make. I checked Fattoush out in Sophie Grigson's *Eat Your Greens* and in her mum's book *Jane Grigson's Vegetable Book*. She got her version from Claudia Roden's *A Book of Middle Eastern Food*. Comparing them with Greg Malouf's recipe in his book *Arabesque* you can see that in each one there are small differences and one or two ingredients more or less. Malouf uses sumac in his which probably makes it closer to the original; on the other hand he also uses balsamic vinegar – so what can you say? They do though all agree that purslane is an essential ingredient. This is my variant on all of theirs.

For six to eight
> *I cucumber, skin and centre seeds removed, chopped small*
> *3-4 medium tomatoes, deseeded, chopped small*
> *1 medium red onion, chopped small*
> *a bunch of purslane (a good handful or so of leaves), chopped*
> *a heart of crisp lettuce, finely chopped*

6 or more radishes, chopped

4 tablespoons fresh parsley, chopped

2 tablespoons fresh mint, chopped

2 tablespoons fresh coriander, chopped

1-2 garlic cloves, crushed in a little sea salt

olive oil

lemon juice

a little runny honey

a sprinkling of sumac (optional)

Dice the cucumber and sprinkle with a little sea salt. Leave in a colander for 30 minutes, then rinse under running water, spread on kitchen roll and rub dry.

Mix together all the ingredients apart from the garlic, oil, lemon and honey. These are for the dressing; make it fairly lemony but add a touch more honey if it is really sharp. Bear in mind though that the dressing needs to be quite intense. Once it is added to the salad the liquid from the tomatoes and cucumber will dilute it. Pour over the salad and mix everything together with your hands. Sprinkle with the sumac (if using).

Genuine Fattoush calls for crisp pitta bread to be broken up and mixed into the salad. Pitta bread is hard to obtain in France, so unless I have time to make some I usually have to leave it out.

Sara's Warm Salad

This is an interesting idea. It's a mix of salad ingredients and peas, lightly cooked and served warm. It works very well as a side dish with all barbecued or roast meat. I particularly like it as an accompaniment to succulent pink lamb chops, breaded pork or veal fillets, or grilled skewers of lamb that's been marinaded in a mix of ground fennel and cumin, garlic, oil and lemon juice. It is also a perfect accompaniment to pan-fried cod or Dover sole

For four
>   *450g of young fresh or frozen peas, cooked separately*
>   *25g butter*
>   *1 bunch of spring onions, chopped*
>   *1 clove new garlic, crushed and chopped*
>   *good handful of young purslane – leaves and stalks*
>   *2 small crisp Little Gem lettuce hearts, quartered*
>   *2 ripe avocados, cut chunkily*
>   *1 tablespoon fresh parsley, chopped*
>   *1 tablespoon fresh chervil, chopped*
>   *1 teaspoon fresh mint, chopped*
>   *lemon juice*
>   *sea salt and black pepper*

Cook peas as per normal, drain and refresh.

In a pan large enough to hold everything, melt the butter, add the chopped spring onions, garlic and purslane. Cook gently for a minute or two then add the lettuce. Turn it over to coat it well and cook for a further minute or two. Remove pan from heat and add the cooked peas. When the contents of the pan are just warm, add the avocado. Add the herbs, lemon juice, salt and pepper to taste. Gently mix everything together. Check the seasoning and add more melted butter to finish if necessary.

Serve warm.

CHAPTER 3

With One Bound

Perhaps not with one bound but we did make it with a day in hand. Arranging to meet friends on a specific date in a city a very long way away and choosing to make the journey there by one of the slowest means available might be deemed perverse, to say the least. We do like a challenge though. The twelve-day journey from Cambrai to Strasbourg was what we would call 'steady'. Away at seven in the morning, running non stop all day and only tying up once we arrived at a lock that was closed for the night. Then dinner and bed. So much for all the great meals

I was going to rustle up en route. Some of them did actually get rustled but we were often too tired to appreciate them. In fact the food bought in Cambrai lasted us right through to Strasbourg with only the briefest of stops, at a conveniently situated canal-side supermarket near Nancy, for fresh milk, orange juice and a couple of watermelons.

It got hot, really hot, too hot to want to stop. It is a universal truth that no matter which canal you are on and no matter in which direction you are traveling, the sun will always be beating down upon you from directly overhead. This is a well-known fact. All those beautiful plane trees that Napoleon decreed must be planted along the canal banks to provide shade for the weary traveller are useless. Better to keep on the move, creating your own little breeze, with all hatches, doors and portholes open.

I love barging into cities, especially when we can moor up close to the centre. I can't wait to go back to Paris, Gent or Amsterdam, but Strasbourg, no, it is not for me. It was far too hot to be a tourist and I must admit it all felt a bit anti-climatic after our marathon sprint to get there, so perhaps the fault lay not entirely with Strasbourg.

I had, however, expected great things of the food and wine. And it is great, but at its most basic, it is simply rustic peasant food – and seriously hearty stuff too. However it's not to be sneezed at and had it been the middle of winter, a big dish of sauerkraut, Strasbourg sausage, ham hock and sundry other bits of pig, plus the potatoes, would have gone down a treat. I could easily imagine tucking into just such a meal were I ever to spend a day on a snow laden mountainside, in a forest, chopping wood and loading it into wagons. But, this is not food for people with not a lot to do in high summer and with temperatures up in the 30s. 'Ah ha,' I hear the more knowledgeable muttering, 'but what about that other famous speciality of the region: *flammekueche*? That's very good, isn't it?' True, this cream, onion and bacon tart can be quite delicious. It is the Alsatian equivalent of Italian pizza but much lighter and (I think) nicer. We were really looking forward to trying it. Sadly, the first one we ate was horrible, having been utterly debased by some craven spiv whose only intent was to extract cash from the pockets of gullible tourists. The cold, dry, paper-thin base, which should have been warm and soft, so you can roll the whole thing up into a sort of edible cigar, looked and tasted like mouldy cardboard; the cream topping was sour and runny, and the bacon, cheap processed ham. However, given the strength of its reputation, we knew that it had to taste better than that, and so we decided to give it a second innings. The next *flammenkueche*, eaten seated in the shade of a giant plane tree next to the river Ill in the old part of Strasbourg, was quite excellent; with a fresh green salad and washed down with plenty of cold Reisling wine, it made a perfect hot weather lunch and, sitting there, I was reminded of just how good life can sometimes be.

What else? We had great ice-cream from Christian's in the rue Mercière – the best I've eaten outside of Paris. It's a fashionable *salon de thé* with fabulous cakes and tarts and much frequented by the classier Strasbourg ladies. Needless to say we didn't go in (boating doesn't equip one for the standard of elegance required), but happily queued for ages on the pavement for our ice-cream cornets: *'deux boules, s'il-vous-plaît.'*

Several big markets are held on different days throughout the week and in various parts of the city. We only went to one; it was the closest to where we were moored, near the cathedral, quite small, and a true farmers' market of local producers. Cherries and blackcurrants were at their very best. The cherries needed only to be run under the tap and put in a bowl on the table in the wheelhouse – they soon disappeared. The blackcurrants I made into intensely zingy sweet-sharp jellies. I gave them an added boost with a spoonful or two of crème de cassis. They set to a gentle wobbliness and needed only a thin layer of fresh cream on top to finish. So good.

I was much taken by the local fennel, smaller and greener than the usual commercial Italian type and sold in bunches. There was also a man selling duck stuff. This region is famous for its foie gras but it was far too hot to be seriously interested. He did have these very nice-looking little duck pancake things for sale. They seemed to be made with shredded duck confit inside a thin batter coating. All you had to do was crisp them up in a pan and they were ready to serve. We ate them with a salad of lentils and some figgy balsamic dressing.

The real find though, was the little jars labelled *'Ail des Ours'* – bear garlic. The jars were filled with a dark green shredded leaf, lightly salted and mixed with olive oil. I was intrigued, especially when the stall-holder opened a jar and gave me a taste; the leaf looked like spinach but was quite crisp and very garlicky. Further discussion established that these were indeed leaves that were gathered in the countryside in spring. We call them ramsons or wild garlic. Although I have often picked this fresh to use raw in salads when we find it in England, it had never occurred to me that one might make a preserve out of it. So I bought a couple of jars. It's good used like pesto with pasta, or added to a vegetable soup and a little mixed into warm white beans is very tasty. I can't wait for when I shall be able to pick and make my own preserve; it likes to grow in damp shady places in woods or near the water's edge and should not be too hard to find.

So thank you Strasbourg for the great ice-cream and the *ail des ours*. Now though, we have decided to retrace our steps – if such a thing is possible in a boat – heading back towards the Champagne region. We can enjoy boating at a much more leisurely pace, stopping at some of the places we swished through on the way here. No rush then – but I've no doubt that my Captain will be up at six tomorrow morning, the engine will burst into life sometime around seven and Strasbourg will be but a fading memory at five minutes past.

Saverne is hardly a day's run from Strasbourg but we had booked dinner at a restaurant there and a prompt arrival would allow us time to explore the town and to get spruced up for our meal. We were looking forward to eating at this restaurant as it had been mentioned to us by several people and had a good write-up in both the Guides Michelin and Gault Millau.

The approach to Saverne by canal is very impressive and it is clearly a popular stopping spot. The port is full of boats, both private and with a base for holiday hire. So long is the frontage that there is even a spot at one end reserved for boats of our sort of size, though on this particular day, sadly, already full. On the opposite bank is the huge summer palace, built back in the 1740s for Cardinal Louis de Rohan, which means there is even something quite interesting to look at once you have moored up and are sitting on deck sipping your congratulatory glass of vino. Congratulations for what, you might ask? Well, just for being there really. Anyway in view of the lack of space and therefore no immediately forthcoming glass of said vino, we decided to continue on through the lock and stop somewhere above it.

Saverne must once have been a far busier and more industrious town than it is today. The local population would have had better things to do than hang around locks and travellers would have just got on with their traveling. Not so nowadays. The lock in Saverne is slap bang in the very centre of the town. Each time a boat arrives, it is immediately surrounded by what, in UK canal parlance, are known as 'gongoozlers' – people with nothing better to do than watch the boats go by. Now this is something we are very used to: when we worked narrowboats on English canals, even in mid-winter, in the dark and in the middle of nowhere, as soon as we hove into sight, a few people would always appear and gather round the lock. In those days, it took us about four minutes to work through one; this from the time we entered the lock to when we left it. And we worked the locks ourselves, running around, shutting gates, lifting paddles and attending to the boats. Should the said gongoozlers want to chat there were only moments in which to do so before we were out of the lock and on our way again.

At Saverne it is quite different. This lock has an impressive rise of some 5.5 metres and works automatically at the pull of a lever; no need therefore to even step off the boat. And because it is the very first one that many people just starting out from Saverne on their hire boat holiday will have encountered, and being unusually deep for a *Freycinet* lock, the mechanism which allows the water in and out is geared to do so at a snail's pace. Which means you – or in this case, we – are condemned to sit in the lock for twenty minutes or more as it fills so slowly as to be barely perceptible. The gongoozlers watch us, massed ranks of them by now, but they are silent spectators. We, it seems, are a little sideshow, a tourist attraction perhaps, and no one actually seems to want to speak to us. They stare at us. I try not to look at anyone and just fiddle with the rope I am holding. At last the lock is nearly full and we have risen to the same level as our audience. There is a final, interminable, deeply embarrassing period while the water in the lock slowly, slowly tries to make a level with the canal on the other side of the gates. It is as though time has stood still. They continue to watch us though studiously avoiding any eye contact. We wait for the gates to open and release us from our ordeal. Will they applaud us when we leave, I wonder? Suddenly recalling those 'Loony Toons' cartoons we used to watch as kids and the way they always ended with the writing appearing on the screen and Bugs Bunny saying 'That's all, folks!', I spend the remaining few minutes practising his silly voice in my head and trying to put the words into French. What is the best translation of 'folks' I wonder? No matter, as it happens my courage fails me at the precise moment and all I can manage is a tiny embarrassed wave, but already the gongoozlers are moving on. It's the end of the show. I'd imagined they might stay and sing 'God save the Queen' to the English barge as it left the lock. Standing and singing the National Anthem was once the normal practice in British cinemas and theatres as the curtain fell, but it was not to be.

There was no-one, thank goodness, to watch us trying to moor up in a really stupid place just around the corner. We finally managed it, Captain having first to work out how I was going get on and off the boat without falling into the canal. Tidied up, we went off to explore Saverne before our restaurant visit. This did not take long. The palace, up close, proved to be an empty, rather ugly, crumbling edifice. It, no doubt, provides a magnificent backdrop to the odd civic event and a certain cachet to the photos of the wedding parties that assemble in front of it, but all in all, nowadays, the Cardinal's old palace must be something of a burden to this little town.

The restaurant 'Staeffele' in rue Pointcaré was more than good enough. The Alsace wines from the restaurant's cellars were so good that we managed to get through a couple of bottles in the course of our meal — all in the line of research, you understand. Although to be honest, I can never quite recall just what it was that we did drink.

Next day as we pass through the top lock onto the summit level, I buy a big bunch of parsley, a pot of honey and some really luscious little strawberries from the lock-keeper. There is a box, left outside his back door, to put the money in if there is no one around. He is in his garden. He gives me a wave but does not bother to leave his hoeing; he feels no need to check on what I am taking nor how much I put in the box.

The Marne Rhine Canal presents one with a treat every few kilometres. Forests climb from the very edge of the water up the sides of steep hills. At any moment I expect to see the famous wild boar that inhabit the woodlands to come slipping and sliding down the slope before plunging into the canal. In some places the waterway has been simply hacked out of the rock and seems to hang at the very edge of a precipice.

We arrive at the inclined-plane boat lift at St Louis-Arzvillers which opened for business in 1969 and carries boats up and down the incline. It was built to replace an earlier flight of some sixteen arduous locks. This incredible device was being operated by two teenage girls whose summer job, it seems, is to press the correct buttons which speed boats in its water-filled caissons willy-nilly up and down the hillside. They seem completely unfazed by this huge responsibility. I look around, hoping vaguely, that somewhere in the background there is a grown-up keeping an eye on them.

We cross the long summit level through miles of seemingly unpopulated countryside, hasten through a couple of tunnels and decide it is time to stop. It is hot, hot, hot. I look at the water longingly. What wouldn't I give just to leap overboard and cool down in these crystal clear waters? When we finally stop at Gondrexange where there are huge lakes on either side of the canal, I do just that. Heaven.

Food-wise we are reduced to eating nothing but simple salads and watermelon. No longer is the fridge packed with wine; instead cold bottles of water have become the priority. The wine is back in the bilges where it belongs. These are well below water level and so keep relatively cool anyway. When we finally leave the peaceful setting of the Etangs de Gondrexange it is only because our water tanks are getting decidedly low and we need to find a tap.

Fresh food is also running out and we are down to whatever I can rustle up from the nether regions of the fridge and store cupboard. There are two little Camembert cheeses beginning to make their presence felt (smelt) from where I have stored them in the cool darkness of the bilges. I have a pack of puff pastry in the fridge, a jar of redcurrant jelly and the parsley bought from the lock-keeper a day or two ago. I decide to make something which, though somewhat 'retro' and rather richer than is wholly good for one, is also totally delicious and decadent and therefore the proverbial 'no brainer' as I believe they say. I'll bake the cheese in the pastry and serve it with warm redcurrant jelly. The parsley leaves, I'll deep fry to a crispy frizzle. Encircling the pastry on the plate, they not only look inviting, but also add a pleasant, slightly metallic crunchiness to the meal.

We have moored for the night below a lock absolutely in the middle of nowhere. The locks stop working at 7.00 in the evening. As they are automatic they switch themselves off and come on again at 7.00 in the morning. It was around 7.30pm, and just as I had put my two cheese-y puff pastry what-nots into the oven, *Friesland* gave a little lurch. Hardly discernible but Captain and I look at each other; this slight movement of the water tells us that someone is traveling along the pound and it isn't going to be a *plaisance* at this time of night. Sure enough around the turn comes a slow moving, heavily laden barge. We realise the skipper is expecting to stop for the night in the deep water where we are presently moored. It is, of course, no problem for him to tie on the outside of us. Except that we want to leave by 6.30 in the morning to run down to the next lock, to be there waiting when it opens at seven. If we end up on the inside of him, he won't start his engine until this lock springs back into life in the morning, which means we won't get away until he decides he is ready to leave. With such a full load it will take him a good 20 minutes just to move off and get into the lock. As the barge approaches, Captain starts

Friesland's engine and calls the boatman up on the radio to tell him we are pulling out and will tie on his outside. We know immediately from the long pause before he speaks that he is not happy with this arrangement. Will the *plaisanciers* still be asleep and their boat in his way when he is ready to go in the morning, he worries? We start to reassure him but he suggests that the space above the next lock is free and why don't we go on down there now, instead of in the morning, given we are untied and the engine is running. Fine, we say – there's no use arguing with 350 tonnes of loaded boat – and we swing away past him.

What he doesn't know is that our supper, now committed to the oven, will be ready in approximately 35 minutes; that's the same length of time it will take for us to boat to the next lock. It's touch and go, but there is little choice in the matter. As it happens I remove the beautifully crisp golden pastries from the oven just as we come in to moor and leave them to cool down a little while we tie up. I had fried the parsley to a crisp as we came along the pound and left it between sheets of kitchen roll to allow any excess oil to drain away. The table is laid and the redcurrant jelly warmed. Five minutes after we tie up, we sit down to dinner. Captain opens a bottle of Beaujolais, from St Amour, made by our favourite growers there, the Duc family, and…. phew…. once we have settled after our unexpected flurry of activity, all is, again, well in our little world.

RECIPES

Alsace and Lorraine are unusual regions of France; close to the Rhine and edged by the Vosges mountains, like most places that find themselves on the boundaries between peoples, these regions have more than their fair share of savage history from before the time of Joan of Arc, born in the village of Domrémy in Lorraine, right through to the bloodiest battles of the First World War at Verdun. Those who survived were tough and strong-minded; they guarded their past and held firm to their traditions and this is reflected in the food, which is bold and substantial. I love the country soup called Soupe au Lard. It's made with bacon and is ideal boating food, containing unfussy ingredients, and once all have been added, can be left to simmer unattended over a low flame while I get on with boat-y jobs outside, such as deck-swilling and the like. Here is simple food that makes a perfect ending to a long day on the move.

Bacon Soup

This peasant soup can be enriched with a good spoonful of double cream at the end of the cooking time making it even more of a dish. Without this addition it is still very good and some may prefer the less rich version.

For six

> *6 slices of fat smoked bacon*
> *1 medium Savoy cabbage*
> *500g butter beans, previously soaked for several hours in cold water*
> *6 leeks*
> *6 carrots*
> *500g small waxy potatoes (Charlottes are perfect)*
> *250g small round onions (those used for pickling are ideal)*
> *1 large onion, halved and stuck with a clove*
> *double cream (optional)*

6 thickish slices of bread (a sourdough loaf is best)
sea salt and freshly ground black pepper

I prefer to make this in my heavy cast iron casserole dish but any large pot with a lid which will hold the contents will do.

Lay the bacon slices in the bottom of the pot and cover with about 4 litres of cold water. Bring this slowly to the boil. Skim off any rising scum from the surface and leave to cook gently for about 20 minutes.

Prepare the cabbage by discarding the outer leaves, cutting it in half and rinsing it well in cold water. Drain the beans, discard the dark green leaves of the leeks, peel and scrape the carrots and potatoes, peel the little onions.

Peel the larger onion, cut it in two and lay both halves directly onto the gas hob or electric hotplate and cook for about 3 minutes. Detach them using a palette knife – they should be slightly burned.

Put the onion halves in the casserole with the cooked bacon, add the beans and simmer for around 30 minutes. Then add the carrots and cabbage and cook gently for a further 30 minutes, skimming the surface from time to time. Add the leeks, potatoes and small onions, taste and salt if necessary and a few twists of black pepper. Cook for a further 40 minutes. Add the double cream (if using) at the end of the cooking time and stir in gently to amalgamate.

Toast the bread to a light golden colour.

Place the toast in a soup tureen or similar and pour over most of the broth. Put the beans, bacon and vegetables in another deep dish with the rest of the broth. Serve them together at the table making sure that both bowls of food plus the dishes you are serving it in are all nice and hot.

Baeckenoffe

This delicious meat and potato stew is an old-established speciality of the region. The word *'baeckenoffe'* means 'the baker's oven' and this is where, in earlier times, this dish would be baked. Traditionally, Monday, almost the world over, was washing day. Dealing with the weekly wash of a large peasant family could take several hours in the communal wash house, the women scrubbing clothes with household soap, rinsing them and squeezing out excess water before hanging everything out to dry. No time therefore to prepare and cook the main midday meal. Instead the meat must be prepared on the Sunday night and then left to marinate until the following morning. Early the next day all the ingredients would be layered into a large earthenware pot and carried down to the village baker. His oven would remain hot for hours after the bread baked that day was removed, and it was into this slow oven that the sealed pots of *baeckenoffe* would be placed, there to slowly cook until noon. Likely then, one of the children would be dispatched to collect the pot and bring it to the waiting family's table.

This traditional recipe from Anne Willan's *French Regional Cooking* is deeply flavoursome, yet an easy dish to make well in advance when you are expecting a crowd.

For six to eight
> *750g boned pork loin, cut into 5cm cubes*
> *750g boned shoulder of lamb, cut into 5cm cubes*
> *750g lean stewing beef, cut into 5 cm cubes*
> *30g lard, dripping or duck fat*
> *2 large onions, thinly sliced*
> *2kg of potatoes, thinly sliced*
> *sea salt and ground black pepper*
> *400ml water, more if needed*
> *luting paste (see below)*

For the marinade
> *2 carrots, thinly sliced*
> *2 onions, thinly sliced*

2 cloves garlic, peeled and crushed
3 cloves
a bouquet garni of parsley, thyme and a bay leaf
750 ml dry white wine preferably an Alsace riesling or sylvaner
sea salt and freshly ground black pepper

Put the pork, lamb and beef in a large bowl (not aluminium) with the other marinade ingredients. Cover and leave to marinate overnight in the refrigerator. Next day remove the meat from the liquid, preserving the marinade.

Melt the lard in a casserole, add the onions and cook over a low fire, stirring occasionally, until they begin to brown; remove the pot from the heat. Put half of the sliced potatoes in a layer over the onions, then put the marinated meat on top; season lightly with salt and pepper. Cover the meat with the remaining potato slices and season again. Strain the marinade over the meat and vegetables and add enough water to come just below the topmost layer of vegetables.

Set the oven to moderately low (165C/Gas 4).

Seal the gap between the casserole and lid with the luting paste. (Luting paste: put about 100 g of flour and 60ml of water in a bowl and stir to make a soft paste. Don't beat or the paste will become elastic and shrink during cooking).

Heat the casserole gently on a low heat on top of the stove for 10 to 15 minutes, then place in the oven to cook for a further 3 to 4 hours. Don't try to open the casserole once it has been sealed; the meat should cook slowly and in an even heat. When the cooking time is complete, break the seal and discard the luting paste. Serve the meat and vegetables directly from the casserole.

This is a dish that requires a load of hungry people around the table. The glorious smell that rises from the casserole as the luting paste is broken away and the lid is lifted has everyone looking like that old advert for Bisto – their noses stuck up into the air, eyes closed and beautific smiles on their faces. Dish out into big bowls with plenty of country sourdough bread to hand.

Leek Tart

Quiche Lorraine originated from this area of eastern France and whilst I do enjoy it, I much prefer the lesser known Tarte aux Poireaux, not least because the leek is a hugely popular vegetable, found in every market in the land; it deserves its moment in the limelight and this tart is it.

For six

    600g leeks
    1 medium onion
    40g butter
    100g thinly sliced smoked streaky bacon, thinly sliced, cut into small pieces
    2 egg yolks
    1 teaspoon cornflour
    300ml crème fraîche
    150g grated Gruyère cheese, grated
    sea salt and freshly ground black pepper
    grated nutmeg

Pastry

    225g plain flour
    100g salted butter
    1 small glass of iced water

First make the pastry. You can always use good quality bought pastry but with the aid of a food processor it takes mere moments to make the pastry at home. Just throw in the sifted flour and the butter chopped into small pieces with just enough water to process the mix into a ball. Wrap in cling film and leave in a cool place for at least an hour.

Otherwise sift the flour onto a wooden board. Cut the butter into small pieces and scatter over the flour. Make a well in the centre of the flour and pour in a little iced water. With cool hands and working quickly, work the butter into the flour, then draw the butter and flour into the water until a smooth dough is formed. Knead a few times with the palms of the hands, shape into a ball and leave covered in a cool place for at least an hour. Don't worry if you can still see bits of butter dotted about in the pastry.

Preheat the oven to 190C/Gas 5

Roll out the pastry and line a 30cm pie dish, cover and refrigerate.
Trim the leeks, discarding the tough green leaves but leaving as much tender green as possible. Wash them under running water, slice them downwards and then into short oblong pieces. Pat dry with a clean tea cloth.

Peel and thinly slice the onion.

Melt the butter in a large saucepan, add the leeks and onions. Put on the lid and leave to sweat gently over a low heat. Stir from time to time until they are nearly tender and any liquid has evaporated. Add the chopped bacon and cook for a further 5-6 minutes until the bacon is transparent.

In another bowl beat the egg yolks with the cornflour and the crème fraîche. Add the grated cheese, salt and pepper and a grating of nutmeg.

Make sure there is absolutely no liquid left in the leek and onion mixture. If there is quickly cook it off at a high heat. Then add the egg and crème fraîche mixture to the leeks away from the heat. Mix well and check the seasoning.

Pour the mixture into the prepared pastry case and bake in the oven for about 30 minutes.

Serve immediately as it is not a tart that benefits from being made in advance and reheated.

We have this often for lunch with a fresh green salad. If I am doing a simple midday meal for a couple of friends then I'll make a light soup as a starter, followed by the leek tart, finishing with fresh goats' cheese and whatever fruit is to hand – cherries are particularly nice.

Camembert in Puff Pastry

This is so indulgent but it could be argued that the act of boating, which can be steady physically active work all through the day, is sufficient justification for making it once in a while. Ideally I like to use quite small Camembert cheeses to make this so that each person has their own individual one surrounded by a ring of bright green parsley. Cutting into the golden pastry crust releases the hot creamy lava onto the plate. It also means no fighting over the lovely crisp parsley. The little Camemberts are not too easy to find so this recipe assumes two people sharing one pie.

For two
    375g pack all-butter puff pastry
    plain flour, for dusting
    250g whole round Camembert
    1egg, beaten
    a huge bunch of curly parsley
    jar of redcurrant jelly

Heat oven to 220C/Gas 7.

Halve the pastry, then roll out each half into a round on a lightly floured surface to about the thickness of a £1 coin. Sit the cheese on top of one round leaving at least a 4cm surround of pastry.

Brush the pastry around the cheese with some beaten egg. Place the second round of pastry on top and gently mold over the cheese, squeezing out the air as you go, then seal it all the way around the edge. Use scissors to cut away excess pastry, leaving about a 4cm border around the cheese. Use the prongs of a fork to press the edges – this looks pretty and seals the pastry even more. Lift onto a baking tray lined with baking parchment. Make a small hole in the top to let steam out as it cooks and, if you feel like it, cut out some little pastry leaves to surround it. Brush all over with beaten egg. Bake for 20-25 minutes until the pastry is golden, crisp and well risen around the edges. Wait for 5 mins before cutting.

To make the fried parsley:

To minimise the danger of any splashing fat I use a wok to fry the parsley in. Pour in vegetable oil to a depth of about 2.5cm. Heat to sizzling.

From a big – I mean really big – bunch of curly parsley remove the leaves and any little sprigs. Put a couple of handfuls of the leaves into a steel mesh long-handled sieve (the type that you would use to sieve flour through) and carefully lower it into the hot fat. It will sizzle wildly for a moment and the parsley will immediately turn a darker green and crisp up. This will only take a few seconds providing the oil is hot enough. Tip out and spread it onto sheets of absorbent kitchen roll to remove the excess fat. Continue frying the parsley in small batches until you have enough to encircle the pastry when it is on the plate.

To make the redcurrant jelly sauce:

Another store-cupboard item. You can use it direct from the jar but I prefer it warm and slightly less solid. So put a couple of good tablespoons of the jelly into a small saucepan. Add two tablespoons of water and heat gently, stirring and mixing the two until it has become more of a pouring sauce.

Serve the Camembert pie on warm plates surrounded by the crisp parsley with a jug of the redcurrant sauce on the side.

Wild Garlic Preserve

One of the best known ways to preserve wild garlic leaves is to prepare a simple pesto. Bear in mind its season is very short, so make several pots to keep you going.

For every 100 grams of wild garlic leaf, you will need 1 tablespoon of olive oil and half a teaspoon of sea salt .

Thoroughly wash the leaves in plenty of cold water. Put the leaves between two clean tea towels and rub them gently to dry. Place all three ingredients in a food mixer. Chop the leaves finely but do not over process.

Fill small sterilised pots with the preserve leaving 1cm of space at the top. Cover with a layer of olive oil. I usually have one in the fridge and the rest in a freezer or they will keep well for a few weeks stored somewhere cool and dark. In my case – *Friesland's* bilges.

Blackcurrant Jelly with Cassis and Cream

Why ever do people scoff at jelly? It can be such a deliciously light summery dessert. I love serving it to French guests when we are in France. The nearest they ever seem to get to jelly in their own cookery are the solidified juices which naturally accumulate around a meat pâté or the rather old-fashioned dishes that employ a savoury aspic. They are not familiar with sweet dessert jellies, so it is another dish that one can serve as something 'typically British'.

I was so torn when I saw all those wooden punnets of freshly cropped blackcurrants in the market at Strasbourg. For a moment I contemplated making my own crème de cassis with them but luckily came quickly to my senses. This is not something you want to be doing on a boat and in a heat wave. Instead I imagined how deliciously sharp and refreshing a cool blackcurrant jelly would be. The tartness is cut by the addition of a little Védrenne cassis* and softened with a layer of thin cream on top. Serve it with a shortcake biscuit or two on the side.

For four

> *250g blackcurrants*
> *4½ sheets gelatine*
> *500ml water, plus extra for soaking the gelatine*
> *80g caster sugar*
> *50ml crème de cassis*

First of all pick out four perfect little bunches of blackcurrants and keep to one side.

Put the leaves of gelatine in a bowl of cold water to soften.

Swill the rest of the blackcurrants in some cold water, removing any stalks and leaves. This is easily done by taking each bunch of currants and running a fork down the stem to separate them from it. Put the berries in a stainless-steel saucepan. Add the 500ml of water and sugar and bring to the boil.

When the blackcurrants have started to burst, pour them into a sieve lined with a square of damp muslin set over a jug or bowl and leave them to drip through for 10 minutes or more. If you want your jelly to be reasonably clear resist pressing the berries down to extract the last of the juice. Remove the softened gelatine from the water and drop into the warm blackcurrant juice, stirring until it has dissolved.

Allow the jelly mixture to cool a little before adding the crème de cassis. Divide the jelly between 4 individual glass bowls, cover and allow to cool. Leave to lightly set for about 4 hours in the fridge.

To serve: run a layer of thin cream over the top of the jelly. Dip the little bunches of blackcurrants into some caster sugar to lightly coat. Place one bunch on top of each cream-covered jelly.

This recipe is equally good using blueberries instead of blackcurrants. I save enough of the best fresh berries to drop about a dozen into each bowl. Pour on the jelly and leave to set. The blueberries burst in the mouth and add a sharp fruitiness to the dessert.

(*See My Store Cupboard Favourites, p.239)

CHAPTER 4

I Love Nancy

The timing of our arrival at Nancy was not great – late Saturday afternoon after all the shops had shut and with not a lot in the cupboard for the weekend. So once *Friesland* was settled into her mooring in the port, we set off to see what we could find.

We discovered that on Sunday mornings there is a little food market in the Grande Rue, thus was one problem solved. For our immediate sustenance, all that was required was a quick perusal of our foodie bibles, the Gault Millau and Michelin guides, to see what Nancy might have to offer us on the gastronomic front on a Saturday night.

The Sunday food market was small but sufficient. We found it surrounded by antique and bric à brac stalls which was a bonus because I like poking around at such things. A milk jug took my fancy – it would be our souvenir from Nancy. The next few days were spent exploring the town with frequent stops at one of the numerous cafés in the beautiful Place Stanislas for morning coffee or in the heat of the afternoon a refreshingly sharp, mouth puckering, citron pressé. On the Thursday, just before we planned to leave and on a last visit into town, we found a huge covered food market – three great halls filled to overflowing with everything from common old cabbages to very classy caviar. Several of the stalls had small eating places attached and these, it transpired, are very popular lunch-time places with the locals. The menus change daily and many of the dishes chalked up on the *ardoise* are quite unusual and inventive. 'Next time, next time,' we say to each other.

With water tanks topped up and a fridge full of mismatched delicacies from the covered market, we waved goodbye to the *bateliers* who had made us welcome in their port and were soon, once again, barging through the depths of the countryside; nothing but rolling hills, small streams, stands of woodland, fields of wheat and barley and maize – so restful after the hubbub of the town. The farmers are out in the fields on their huge machines, harvesting the grain; a slight nod of acknowledgement, made in our direction from the driver in his cab as we pass by, our only human contact.

It is strange to be so close to the land and its business, yet engaged in an activity which keeps us so far apart from it. This disconnection can be even more pronounced when boating through the centre of a town or city. I recall the dreamlike quality of the journey along the canal St Martin in the middle of Paris. It is a splendid canal with deep mossy-sided locks, little Eiffel iron footbridges spanning the lock approaches, and huge plane trees that form a shady archway over the water. This is the canal where in 1938, Marcel Carné made the film 'Hôtel du Nord' – still a classic of French cinema. The hotel, the facade anyway, is still there at 102, Quai de

Jemmapes and the whole area has that black and white thirties film set feel to it. Not only do we seem to be caught in a time-warp but it is as though there is a glass wall between us on our barge and the antlike activity on either side of the canal. Everyone is going about their own business, totally engrossed in their own lives, and no one notices us as we pass by. Even weirder is when we leave the last lock in the flight of four and enter the tunnel which runs below the 11th arrondissement to the port of the Arsenal. This particular tunnel is really special. It passes directly beneath the Bastille. Parisian life proceeds apace above whilst we burrow along below. To add to the whole illusory quality, the spotlights in the tunnel create shimmers of rainbow colours that sweep across the roof, illuminating the darkness. At regular intervals there are brick air vents through which sunshine and water filters down. Circles of light shine through the swathes of trailing plants that grow down through the vents. These vertical gardens are reflected in the water in front of the boat and the creepers hang down far enough to brush our wheelhouse roof as we pass beneath.

The idea of barges traveling underground has always struck me as a very odd idea and moves into the realms of the surreal on our arrival at the tunnel of Mauvages. It is nearly five kilometres long and a tug is supposed to be waiting to take us in tow. No tug today we are told. Instead here is a boy on a bicycle who will chaperone you through, *monsieur et madame*. We wonder why we need a boy on a bike. He is no replacement for a tug and clearly does not expect to be pulling us anywhere. No, we are to proceed through under our own power and he will accompany us. In the event of an accident he will be ready to dash off on said bicycle to alert the authorities. We try to follow this weird train of thought but decide not to question it knowing that the conversation will inevitably end with the habitual French shrug. As it happens, once in the tunnel our young chaperone finds that wobbling slowly along beside the boat (there is a towpath) is not much fun. He rides off into the darkness and we never see him again.

My cogitations on the oddness of it all eventually end when we finally drop down through the last lock on this canal onto the Moselle river. Now *Friesland* is in her element; the waterway is wide and deep and full of great big barges. At least here we have lock-keepers to call up on the radio and boats to wave to – we are all part of the same world, understanding more or less what is going on.

Were it not for the fact that we had some business to attend to in Toul and must stop there for a day or two, I cannot imagine why anyone would ever want to. The trip round the town was short. Nowhere obvious to eat other than a couple of pizza places, not much in the way of shops and the midweek market miles away from the boat. But like everywhere else we have ever stopped, it had its saving graces – you just had to go look for them. As it happens they turned out to be quite near at hand. Across the road from our mooring and quite close to the railway station was a little restaurant – 'Chez Victor'. Unprepossessing on the outside and sporting a singularly long menu in the window, something to be regarded with suspicion, we dismissed it. Later though, in desperation, having found nowhere in town to eat, we booked a table for that evening; the only diners – just us and some other people also passing through on the canal. Inside Chez Victor all was set out in simple bistro style with starched white cloths on the tables. The floor was an old-fashioned patterned tile and our little waitress clattered backwards and forwards across it at high speed. The food was simple French and very good. I had a salad of scallops while Captain had the house foie gras. We ate carefully cooked juicy pink kidneys in a mustard sauce, with some spinach and a baked potato. The jug of house red, a light Alsace pinot, was perfectly acceptable. The chef produced a delicious Grand Marnier soufflé to round off our meal. Good coffee to finish and best of all, but a mere step across the road, our barge and bed.

And that is not all.

We had planned to leave the next day, a Sunday. Someone in the port had mentioned that there was the tiniest of farmers' markets, held on a Sunday morning, and just down the road from where we were moored. Forever hopeful we set off to look for it. Sure enough, in a little square off the main street, we found a *crèmerie* stall selling goats' cheeses, crème fraîche, eggs and, to my surprise, just picked myrtles. The local vegetable grower had lettuce, tomatoes, basil and parsley, potatoes, leeks and some nice green beans. I spy tiny Charentais melons and buy two. Plenty there for me to play with. I'll do something interesting with the cheese and tomatoes and I'll use the myrtles to have another go at making a wobbly, fruity, purple jelly. The other stall sold chickens, dead ones I'm glad to say, though still complete with heads and feet and innards. Proper French ladies would not dream of letting anyone else prepare their chicken for cooking. I, being British, city bred and somewhat squeamish, am more than content to let the chicken seller do it for me, which she does quickly and with satisfying expertise. Beheaded and befooted, gutted and trussed, she hands it over with a smile, along with a little plastic bag containing liver, heart and gizzard. These, roasted alongside the chicken, are the cook's perks, to be consumed in the kitchen, Keith Floyd style, with a goodly slurp of the cooking wine (best quality of course).

And that is not all.

On the way back from the market we stopped at the baker's; it was barely a hop across the road from the small port in which we were moored. We bought some quiche for lunch, bread for later, a hazelnut meringue and as a special Sunday treat, some flan to have with coffee later in the afternoon, once we were underway. Now Captain is a bit of a flan aficionado. For those unfamiliar with French custard tart – totally unlike our English one – this has a custard filling reminiscent of very solid old-style Bird's custard. It is poured into a thin pastry case and lightly coated with syrup so the top browns as it cooks. Every French baker sells flan. It is very old fashioned and its quality highly variable. The pastry can be too thick in proportion to the amount of custard or too thin and therefore hard and dry. Occasionally the custard filling is sickly sweet and tastes of undercooked cornflour. Mostly, they are just fairly run of the mill. This one, he declared, was the best he had ever tasted, and for a moment we considered turning the boat round and going back for more. Too late of course, we were miles away, and anyway being Sunday they would have closed by now.

The water was incredibly clear. We could see everything growing in the canal and literally hundreds of fish, some, enormous. The bottom of the canal was pristine and quite free of the supermarket trolleys, car tyres, dumped motorbikes and defunct white goods that lurk on the bed of many British canals just waiting to ensnare any unwary boat. After passing the turnoff for the Meuse, the more popular route to the North, it being a river with far fewer locks, we were on our own.

The Marne-Rhine Canal is very beautiful, though heavily locked. In the days when it was considerably busier, so many hand operated locks must have slowed traffic down to a wearisome crawl. Now as we begin the long climb up to the next summit level a very old lady living in one of the lock houses hobbles out to chat. She tells us how lonely it is there nowadays. Just when the canal authorities had finally automated all the locks, which could now be worked from the boat with a zapper, the working barges had all gone and with the automation, the lock-keepers too. Those who now lived in the lock-side cottages were long retired. As we rise up in the lock she hands me down a few flower sprigs from the shrub growing beside her door. 'Hortensia,' she says and shuffles back inside.

It is hard to see how keeping such waterways open can be justified with virtually no commercial traffic and pleasure boats so thin on the ground. If it were easier to tie up somewhere pleasant, albeit in the middle of nowhere, more pleasure boats might be encouraged to come this way. We stop at the occasional derelict wharf out in the country or tie to trees when we can get anywhere near the bank. There are many times when all you want to do is moor somewhere peaceful, go for a walk, swim in the canal, watch the birds, read a book – even try to write one. I love the utter peacefulness of it all. This feeling of well-being continues: there's no excitement, no alarums or excursions, no Internet connection, absolutely nothing happening, and while it might not make for exciting copy, this is exactly how we like our boating to be.

RECIPES
Goats' Cheese, Basil and Tomato Starter

This is an easily made tasty starter for a dinner for four, or you can serve it in very small amounts as an *amuse bouche*. We have no trouble eating this much between the two of us for lunch. Although at its best made with fresh market produce, it works pretty well even if you have to buy your cheese in a supermarket and use tinned tomatoes.

We first had something like this for lunch in a little wine bar which we visit occasionally when we are in Mâcon.

For four as a starter
> *4-6 ripe tomatoes, ideally Coeur de Boeuf, Andine Cornue or the long Italian ones, skinned, de-pipped and well chopped (or a good quality tin of peeled quarters)*
> *about a dessertspoon of runny light flavoured honey*
> *Maldon sea salt and freshly ground black pepper to taste*

Worcester Sauce

250g very young, fresh, soft goats' cheese

cold pressed extra virgin olive oil (your best)

2 tablespoons (at least) of fresh basil leaves, well chopped

1 clove of garlic crushed, finely chopped

a dash of lemon juice

4 tablespoons pesto

Remove the stalks from the tomatoes and cut a little cross in their place. Place the tomatoes in a bowl and pour boiling water over them. Leave for a minute or two then drain and cover with cold water. Drain off the water and the tomatoes should peel easily. Cut them in two and remove pips and juice with your fingers, also any hard inner core. Roughly chop the flesh, lightly salt it and leave to drain in a wire sieve. If using canned tomatoes with skin and seeds already removed, all you now need to do is chop and salt them and leave to drain. Ideally for an hour or more. Give them a gentle press with the back of a wooden spoon every so often to help release as much juice as possible. Keep the juice and use it for cold tomato consommé or a (not very) bloody Mary.

Once the tomatoes are drained, put them in a bowl and add the honey – a little at a time; balance it with salt, pepper and a few drops of Worcester sauce. Do this as though you were an alchemist – a little of this, a little of that and taste, taste, taste. Once it tastes good to you, put the tomato mixture back in the sieve to drain some more and leave to one side.

In a bowl, mix the cheese with olive oil until it is the consistency of clotted cream. Add the basil and chopped garlic. Mix well. Taste, add salt if necessary, pepper and a little lemon juice. Leave to stand for at least 30 minutes or longer if you can, to let all the flavours meld together.

Serve this, ideally, in four small straight sided glasses. Place a quarter of the goats' cheese in the bottom, cover with a thick layer of tomato and finish with a small dollop of pesto on the top and a sprig of basil. In summer, serve straight from the fridge.

A Warm Goats' Cheese Salad

Conscious as I am of all those who screw up their noses in distaste at any mention of goats' cheese, I also know how many have thoroughly enjoyed eating my *salade de chèvre chaud*, albeit without knowing that it is made with the aforementioned 'orrible stuff. This salad appears in some shape or form in virtually any bistro or brasserie you care to visit in France and is the ideal simple lunch, especially when accompanied by a cold glass of youthful Beaujolais. It was once about all you would be offered to eat outside of Paris if you were vegetarian. There are plenty of other tasty ways of using goats' cheese and as it is a ubiquitous feature in every French market it is well worth persuading your nearest and dearest to develop a taste for it.

This salad works best with firm rounds of cheese: semi mature *crottins* somewhere between youthful freshness and mature pungency. You can also use a *bûche* or log-shaped cheese from which you can cut the rounds. My own take on this salad has a slightly autumnal feel as I like to make it when the walnuts begin to fall and figs and apples ripen. The salad base I prefer is a mix of baby spinach, lambs lettuce and a handful of spicy rocket.

For four

> *200g salad leaves*
> *8 slices of baguette cut to the approximate size of the rounds of cheese*
> *a little walnut oil to drizzle over the baguette slices*
> *300g of medium-ripened goats' cheese*
> *1 large crisp dessert apple, cored, cut into quarters and then thinly sliced*
> *4 ripe figs, each cut into 6 pieces*
> *50g walnuts, slightly broken up*

For the dressing
> ½ *teaspoon Maille mi-forte* Dijon mustard*
> 2 *tablespoons aged balsamic vinegar*
> 1 *teaspoon runny honey*
> 4 *tablespoons walnut oil*
> *sea salt and freshly ground black pepper*

Mix the dressing ingredients together tasting as you go until the balance is right.

Put the washed and dried salad leaves in a bowl.

Heat the grill to high.

Slide the baguette slices under the grill and toast one side only. Turn over and drizzle on some walnut oil. Place a round of cheese on top of each piece of baguette and replace under the grill for a couple of minutes until the surface of the cheese is colouring here and there and bubbling. (I put them on a sheet of tinfoil – less mess).

Pour a small amount of the dressing onto the salad leaves and mix gently by hand so that they are very lightly coated. Divide them between 4 plates and scatter over the apple, figs and walnuts. Set two cheese topped baguette rounds on each plate and finish with a drizzle of dressing over the salad.

(*See My Store Cupboard Favourites, p.236)

Melon with Ratafia

The melons you are planning to use must be no larger than a grapefruit (one per person), deliciously ripe and juicy, otherwise there is little point to serving them like this. If you have larger ones then it is better to simply cut the flesh into bite-sized pieces; place on a dish for sharing, with toothpicks to spear them with, and glasses of very cold ratafia on the side. Dip the melon pieces in your glass of ratafia.

Though the usual liquid filling is port wine I prefer the lighter option of ratafia. This is a fortified wine made in the Champagne and Burgundy regions. It is sweet but not overly so. Poured into the centre of a small ripe melon, then left to get really cold, the ratafia mixes with the melon juices and is a delicious but simple starter to a summer meal.

1 small ripe Charentais melon per person
enough ratafia to fill the centre of each melon

Cut out a small circle at the stalk end of each melon, just big enough to insert a teaspoon. Use the spoon to scoop out all the seeds, leaving a cavity in the centre. Fill this full of ratafia (or port), and replace the piece you cut out. Stand each melon in a small bowl or something to keep it upright.

Place in the fridge for at least half-an-hour before serving.

Chicken Breasts Wrapped in Foil

When there are just the two of us I tend to cut a fresh chicken into eight pieces and use them for a couple of different meals. The carcass gets turned into stock and does as a base for a summery soup.

This way of using the two breast fillets is an easy-to-make meal, low in calories, and seriously tasty to boot. I think the idea came originally from Mike Robinson, a British chef, whose home counties country pub is well known for its delicious game dishes.

For two
> *2 skinless chicken breasts*
> *2 medium leeks (white part only), finely chopped*
> *a few slices of thinly sliced prosciutto ham*
> *a glass of dry white wine*
> *a drop of concentrated chicken stock (I like the handy bottled Knorr concentrates**
> > *if I am without any homemade)*
> *a few sprigs of tarragon*
> *2 tablespoons of crème fraîche or double cream*
> *2 squares of tinfoil big enough to comfortably accommodate each chicken piece*

Preheat oven 200C/Gas 6.

Trim the breasts of any fat or sinew. Place a small sprig of tarragon on top of the meat and then wrap each one in some slices of prosciutto. Chop the leeks finely, separating them out slightly so they will cook evenly, and lay them on the tinfoil squares. Place the prosciutto wrapped chicken on top of the leeks with one or two more sprigs of tarragon tucked in top and bottom. Pull up the sides of the tinfoil so that you can pour a good splash of the white wine and a little splash of the concentrated chicken stock into each one. Carefully seal the tinfoil parcels leaving plenty of room inside for the chicken to steam.

Place them in the middle of the preheated oven for about 20 minutes. Check that the breasts are just cooked by piercing with a pointed knife. If cooked the juices will run clear. Remove the parcels from the oven and opening one end carefully drain the liquid from each parcel into a small saucepan. Reseal the parcels and leave them somewhere warm to rest for 10 minutes while you make the sauce.

Heat the chicken liquid and taste. It should be nicely intense in flavour. Pour in the crème fraîche/double cream and mix to make a creamy sauce. Carefully pour a little of the sauce back into each parcel.

I like to serve them with just a few buttery Charlotte potatoes and some green beans. Equally as good and more in keeping with the region try it with the Alsace noodles known as *spaetzli*.

(*See My Store Cupboard Favourites, p.234)

Spaetzli

Typical of the Alsace region and a dish which is made in every home because it is so versatile. These noodles can be served with almost anything, rather like mashed potato, and are equally as good on their own tossed in butter or finished with a simple tomato or mushroom sauce.

For four
>*250g plain flour*
>*4 whole eggs*
>*1 egg yolk*
>*1 tablespoon double cream or crème fraîche*
>*a pinch of salt dissolved in 3 tablespoons water*
>*a small pinch of nutmeg*
>*80g butter*
>*Maldon sea salt and freshly ground black pepper*

Sieve the flour into a bowl. Make a well in the centre and put in all the other ingredients except the butter and seasoning. With your hand or a spatula draw the flour into the centre mixing gently as you do so. Once you have incorporated all the ingredients, work the mixture more vigorously to aerate it and give it some body. The dough should be soft and once it starts to come away from the sides of the bowl stop mixing. Cover the bowl with a damp cloth and refrigerate for around 30 minutes.

Fill a large saucepan with lightly salted water and bring to the boil. Now spread some of the dough onto a small wooden board or similar. With a cold palette knife scrape slivers of the dough into the boiling water. (I have a useful large plastic spoon full of holes. I can fill it with the dough and push it through the holes using the back of another large spoon. I bought it in Nancy, or you can use a potato press if you want.) Cook the noodles in two batches for 3 to 4 minutes until they float to the surface. Skim them out as they rise and put directly into a bowl of cold water.

Drain them well. Heat the butter in a pan and when hot put in the noodles. Move them around to coat all over with the butter and heat through until they are lightly golden. Season to taste and serve at once.

The Rest of the Chicken Baked with Tomatoes

This is one of those meals that is really long-suffering and always willing to wait a bit and is therefore a boon to the distracted boater having trouble finding somewhere to moor for the night. Indeed it's a great dish to make for anyone that wants to get something really tasty onto the table without having to spend too long in the kitchen to achieve it.

For two

    2 tablespoons olive or rapeseed oil for frying

    2 chicken thighs and 2 legs, skin on

    1-2 tablespoons olive oil

    4 medium tomatoes, skins removed and sliced across into two halves (ideally use
        ripe Italian plum tomatoes or French Coeur de Bouef)

    6-8 unpeeled garlic cloves

    1 tablespoon lemon thyme or tarragon, leaves only, well chopped

    Maldon sea salt freshly ground black pepper

Preheat oven 200C/Gas 6

In a pan heat a tablespoon or two of oil (I find a wok is good for this recipe).

When the fat is nice and hot gently put in the chicken pieces and quickly sauté them to a golden brown all over.

Remove from the pan and place in an oven dish just large enough to allow the chicken joints to fit reasonably tightly together. Push the tomato halves and garlic down around the chicken.. Scatter over the chopped herb of your choice – don't mix the two. Pour the olive oil over the tomatoes and season generously with salt and pepper. Cover the dish tightly with tinfoil and place in the preheated oven for 20 minutes. Remove the tinfoil and leave the dish to bake for another 20 minutes until the tomatoes are just beginning to caramelise.

I like this best with a little boiled rice, but it is just as good with a few potatoes or spaetzli.

Myrtles with Meringue and Crème Fraîche

When we are boating I love puddings that take mere moments to put together. I still like a small sweet finish to my meal and any play on the ubiquitous Eton Mess works for me. Among the many bonuses to boating in France is that one can buy airy, freshly baked meringue in most *boulangeries*. They usually come in white or a somewhat garish pink. The pink, I eschew, in favour of the white for this type of dessert. I buy meringue when I see it as it has a very long life on board if kept in a tin in a dry place. Almost any ripe soft fruit, like peaches, apricots, plums, raspberries or, as in this case, blueberries, will do.

With myrtles or blueberries, if I have time and remember to do it in advance so they have time to cool down before I use them, I heat the berries with barely a tablespoon of water and a dessertspoon of sugar until they have softened ever so slightly and are just beginning to release their juices. I remove from the heat at this point as we don't want them cooked through. Once cooled I add a tablespoon or two of crème de mûre or myrtille*, stir it in gently, and leave until it is time to serve.

This is not a dish where you need to carefully calculate the amount and ratio of ingredients. Just lightly crumble crisp meringue into a large bowl. Drain the juice from the blueberries into a jug to serve separately and speedily mix the berries themselves with the meringue. Add lashings of thick crème fraîche bearing in mind that, unlike English double cream, it doesn't really whip. If you have a good high fat one like *Crème d'Isigny* or similar it will whip though it is already quite thick and so can be mixed in directly.

Don't wait – serve it straight away with the jug of 'spiked' juice.

(*See My Store Cupboard Favourites, p.239)

CHAPTER 5

The Perfect Canal

We keep moving on a largely empty canal with few hold-ups, only stopping when we come to a lock that has automatically switched off for the night. This year it is deemed that there will be no headlong rush to Champagne; instead we will boat for fewer hours each day and stop more often and for longer. When we turn up onto the Oise à l'Aisne Canal I vow that it is on this canal that we must stay for a while and re-connect with those places we have so enjoyed exploring over the years. In some ways, for me, it is *the* perfect waterway: the water is deep and clear; each lock works efficiently, is clean and well maintained; the lock houses and their gardens are a joy to behold, though, as it would appear to be the same lock-keeper who takes the 'Best Garden' prize every year, it is surprising that the other contestants don't lose heart. Between locks there is rarely any discernible towpath, which means no fishermen, walkers or cyclists, giving us a feeling of pleasant isolation. The trees reach towards each other on either side of the waterway; the effect is that of passing through a long green tunnel. Wild life abounds: herons, their small fiefdoms marked out, stand patiently beside the water and as we approach, they take off, lazily flapping their way down the canal in front of us; kingfishers are a common sight and the aerial displays of swifts and swallows swooping back and forth after insects, coming in like tiny bombers as they dive low across the boat, hold us entranced. I spend much time and wasted effort out on deck trying to snap the definitive 'heron in flight' picture. As yet, without success, though I am amassing quite an extensive collection of '*bits* of heron in flight'.

On the Oise à l'Aisne there are lots of easy places to tie; places where one can settle quietly for a few days and with some good walks too. We tie as close as we can to Coucy-le-Château. It's a bit of a long walk from the canal (and only a slightly less demanding bike ride) up to this ancient fortified village but really worth the effort. Once the largest defensive structure ever constructed in France, it covered some 14 hectares. The castle of Coucy, built in the 13th century, had 33 towers and ramparts stretching to over two kilometres. The keep was the largest castle tower in Christendom and its inhabitants once the greatest aristocrats in the land. They proudly made their point with the rhyme:

> *roi ne suis,*
> *ne prince ne duc ne comte aussi;*
> *Je suis le sire de Coucy*

('I am not king, nor prince nor duke nor count; I am the Lord of Coucy'.) Sadly Coucy fell into German hands in 1914 and the hill-top fortification and château were occupied by them until 1917. When they left, they pillaged the town and destroyed the castle, using some 25 tons of dynamite to achieve its destruction.

The ruins remain as an impressive reminder of Coucy's past grandeur despite the invaders' efforts to obliterate it completely. Today it is hardly possible to envisage the death and destruction that was once an integral part of this region's past. Now it is little more than a sleepy backwater. There are no major roads or railways nearby and no planes fly overhead. Unlike those who once lived here, the loudest noises we have to complain of are the quacking of ducks and croaking of frogs. At night it is dark and silent and the sky a velvet blanket scattered with diamonds.

A morning is spent exploring the remains of the château and learning more about its inhabitants. We have booked lunch at La Ferme des Michettes just down the road. It has a huge dining room and is clearly geared to receive visitors by the coach load. There is only one set *Menu du Jour* and there's nothing wrong with that as everyone is quickly served, first with a freshly made vegetable soup from huge tureens placed on the tables, followed by plates full of crisp-skinned, spit-roasted *cochon* with a side of potatoes cooked in its dripping juices. The tables are long; jugs of water, bread and huge bowls of dressed salad set out at regular intervals; it has the feel of a monastic refectory. The place fills up, we take our seats and are soon chatting with our fellow diners. Strictly speaking we are still in beer drinking country but the simple wine served with the meal loosens tongues and improves our French no end. After lunch a band arrives and the restaurant is transformed into a *guinguette* – becoming a dance hall with all its aged eaters, including us, taking to the floor. It's odd, it's fun, and very French.

Not only does this canal have plenty of places where a large deep drafted barge like *Friesland* can easily tie, there is even an attractive mooring right outside a most conveniently situated small supermarket. Just because I am a dedicated 'foodie' does not mean I am prepared to forgo a quick forage in one, especially when we can tie up on its doorstep. My objections to them are more to do with how our tastes are shaped to the requirements of the supermarket moguls and the way we are subtly manipulated into buying things we don't want, don't need and can't use. I hate being thought of as 'a consumer' – such a joyless sounding occupation!

At least French supermarkets sell local produce, so help to keep their smaller neighbourhood suppliers in business and support the regional cuisine.

Early on Saturday morning we pull into the mooring close to the bridge leading to the village of Pinon and with shopping list in hand head for the shop entrance. I am immediately diverted from my firm intention to buy nothing but what is on the list. 'That brioche looks nice,' I say, 'we could have it toasted with marmalade when we make our early morning starts and I could make a queen of puddings or we could have pain perdu with some fruit if there is any left over.' In true supermarket fashion the brioche is already sliced and sealed in a plastic bag. It is called *La Gâche:* the blurb tells us it is made with butter, eggs and crème fraîche and I am, of course, seduced into buying it.

Now I will stick to my list ... except here in front of me is huge pile of Charentais melons on special offer and by their warm sweet smell obviously ready to eat right now. I quickly reassess tonight's dinner, which is to be a salad of chicken livers followed by some creamy yogurt, bought from a dairy farm, along with a litre of milk, that we had passed a few miles back. No reason then not to consider a piece of nice ripe melon with some thinly sliced air-dried ham for a simple start to the meal or I could pour the last of a slightly ancient bottle of port over it, then let it get good and cold in the fridge. What could be better than something refreshing and alcoholic at one and the same time? I reason that just one to share between us is worth having if only to use up these odds and ends. I buy two.

'That's it,' I say to my Captain as we walk past the cheese counter. 'Just grab the loo rolls and washing-up liquid and we'll be on our way.' He goes off and I am left looking longingly at the host of cheeses on display. 'Well we could have a smidgin' of Roquefort and maybe that nice little St Marcellin; oh, there's a tasty looking goats' cheese from just down the road, better have some of that by way of giving encouragement to a local producer.' I have little difficulty justifying to myself our need for cheese.

We exit with so much more than I had meant to buy, both shopping list and resolve in tatters. I blame those nasty mind-benders that the supermarket employs; self-control, of course, has nothing to do with it.

On leaving the supermarket mooring we pass an empty *péniche* (working barge) moored up just beyond the bridge. The skipper is clearly taking his summer holiday on his favourite canal too. Table, chairs and umbrella are set up on the grass. There's a ladder tied to the side of his boat so that he and his family can swim in the clear river fed water; his barbecue is alight and is, no doubt, cooking the ready-made brochettes of beef and chicken which I'd spied in the meat section, and being the industrious boatman that he is, he's already been out with the tar varnish and blacked round one side of his barge. He gives us a wave and we wish each other *'bonnes vacances'*.

We head on up towards the summit and yet another nice mooring close to yet another huge reservoir with yet another unpronounceable name – le Lac de Monampteuil. We make good time as all the locks are with us. When we arrive it is deemed too early to stop so we continue through the tunnel down to Bourg-et-Comin. Here we tie up in a peaceful enough spot and put our own table, chairs and barbecue out on the grass beside the boat.

Now what shall we have for dinner?

RECIPES

Melon with Air-dried Ham

Hardly counts as a recipe does it? Rather it's just a shining example of how an unlikely combo of sweet fruit and savoury ham conspire to make something so simple yet so memorable. Set a platter of perfectly ripe Charentais melon slices mixed with slivers of salty, musky air-dried ham on a table, outdoors, on a warm summer evening, offer a view across the water to the fields beyond, and serve it all up with glasses of cold crisp rosé wine. Leave friends to pick at the platter and chatter over the wine while you ease towards a laid-back supper. Simply the best.

Put a few forks on the table so everyone can help themselves. Have plenty in reserve as it will disappear quickly.

Lamb Kebabs

Made in advance and refrigerated until needed, these lamb kebabs can be quickly grilled or cooked on the barbecue. Serve with warm pitta bread. Add a salad of tomatoes, black olives and feta cheese and a big bowl of hummus. Let everyone fill the bread with a mix of salad, meat and hummus. Keep pouring the rosé.

For four
> *1 tablespoon olive oil*
> *4 cloves garlic, crushed*
> *2 teaspoons fresh ginger, grated*
> *4 green chillies, de-seeded and chopped*
> *½ teaspoon black peppercorns, crushed*
> *1 teaspoon ground cumin*
> *½ teaspoon ground coriander*
> *juice from ½ lemon*
> *1 teaspoon Maldon sea salt*

55g fresh coriander leaves, washed and finely chopped
25g fresh mint leaves, washed and finely chopped
450g lamb mince

In a food processor blend to a paste the oil, garlic, ginger, chillies, crushed peppercorns, cumin, coriander, lemon juice, and salt.

In a large bowl mix the paste with the fresh coriander and mint into the minced lamb. Mix really well using your hands. Then with wet hands press the meat into sausage shapes onto long steel skewers. Allow about four kebabs per person per skewer. Alternatively, shape the mixture into flat patties. These can be grilled. Brush each kebab with a little oil and grill under a medium heat or barbecue for 4-5 minutes on each side until cooked through but still nice and juicy.

Grilled or Barbecued Quail

Quail is a very popular little bird in France. They are raised on quail farms in large outdoor enclosures where they are free to run and forage. The runs are covered over with netting to prevent them being carried off by predators. These little birds are ideal for being spatchcocked and grilled, roasted in the oven or cooked quickly on the barbecue. Here's my favourite way of eating them, very basic and simple, indeed it's almost another non-recipe.

For two
4 plump quail
75g butter
2 flattened cloves of garlic
sea salt and freshly ground black pepper
2 tablespoons Dijon mustard
lemon juice

Use kitchen scissors to cut through the backbone longitudinally. Flatten the bird and spatchcock by threading two water-soaked wooden kebab sticks through the flesh to form an 'X'. This will keep the quail flat while they cook.

Melt the butter. Using a pestle and mortar crush the garlic to a paste with a little sea salt, add the mustard and butter and mix well together.

Brush the quail with the melted butter mix and season all over inside and out with salt and pepper. Preheat the grill. Position a sheet of tinfoil which is cut to fit the grill pan, and place the birds on it, breast side down.

Slide the pan under the grill and cook for around 8-10 minutes. Turn the quail breast side up, baste well and squeeze over a generous amount of lemon juice. Cook for a further 8-10 minutes. Check after 5 minutes. If the skin is beginning to burn then place the grill pan on a lower shelf. Baste again and continue grilling until the birds are browned and the skin is nicely crisp.

Provide large napkins (or plenty of kitchen roll) and encourage people to eat with their fingers. Put some good bread on the table to mop up juices and, ideally, serve a peppery watercress salad on the side.

This recipe is easily adapted for cooking outside on the barbecue.

Quick Pain Perdu with Roasted Plums

Having had our fill of early morning toasted brioche and marmalade there are, invariably after a few days, some slightly stale slices left. Making *pain perdu* is a good way of using them up. In fact if we are having some sort of fruit with this dessert and the bread is still soft I make it this quick way – it's just fried bread really – leaving out all the soaking in milk and coating with egg before frying which the normal recipe requires you to do.

For two

> *4-6 large red dessert plums halved and stoned*
> *40g unsalted butter for spreading and to dab onto the plums*
> *50g caster sugar*
> *French quatre-épices powder or Chinese 5-Spice powder*
> *4 slices brioche*

Preheat oven to 200C/Gas 6

Place the halved and stoned plums in an oven proof dish, cut sides facing upwards. (If you have one, use a dish that you can also use on a hob, so that if you need to reduce any liquid to a syrup it can be done in the dish the plums have been baked in.) Dab some butter into each stone hole, liberally scatter with half of the caster sugar and a few pinches of the quatre-épices powder. Pour a little water into the bottom of the dish. Cover with tinfoil and bake in the oven for 20 minutes. Check for doneness. Remove foil and bake for further 5 to 10 minutes. Turn the oven down to its lowest setting. If there is plenty of juice in the dish, reduce it to a syrupy sauce on the hob. Return the dish to oven to keep warm while preparing the pain perdu.

Liberally butter one side of the brioche and sprinkle with a layer of caster sugar. Press the sugar down onto the butter with the flat of a spoon. Heat the grill to medium, lay a sheet of tinfoil over the grill pan and carefully place the slices of buttered brioche upwards on the foil. Slide under the grill, not too close to the heat, as brioche can burn very quickly so you need to keep an eye on it. Continue to toast until the brioche is slightly caramelised. Carefully turn the brioche slices over, butter the second side, sprinkle with sugar and replace under the grill.

Serve two slices per person and top with the plums and a little of the syrup. I like this with a dollop of crème fraîche or better still a helping of caramel ice cream.

My Queen of Puddings

Queen of Puddings is a classic English pudding. Normally it would be layered with jam or a red fruit jelly; I make my own version using a more grown-up orange sauce instead – hence the title 'My' Queen of Puddings. Desserts like this have been around forever because they are a perfect way of using up left-over bread. Nowadays we eat far less bread than in the past so, if I want to make something like this, I have to buy a fresh loaf just to turn into breadcrumbs. Not that I really mind; once I've processed them, which only takes a matter of moments, my mind has already turned to all the other dishes I can make with them: veal escalopes; crown of lamb with a filling of crisp crumbs, garlic and parsley; fennel gratin topped with Parmesan and bread crumbs; extra light dumplings and steamed puddings; treacle tart… and so on and so forth. Fresh breadcrumbs freeze well and can be used straight from the freezer.

For four to six
600ml full-cream milk
thinly sliced peel of half an orange (no white pith)
110g fresh white bread crumbs
50g butter, cut into small pieces and a bit extra for greasing the dish
50g caster sugar
2 medium eggs separated

For the sauce

> *2-3 tablespoons tart marmalade (Bonne Maman Oranges Améres/Bitter*
>   *Orange* is good)*
> *juice 1 orange*
> *dash of Cointreau (or similar)*

Preheat oven to 180C/Gas 4

Pour the milk into a pan and add the orange peel. Bring slowly to the boil then remove from the heat and leave to one side for 15 minutes or so.

Place the breadcrumbs, the butter and half the sugar into a bowl. Add the milk poured through a sieve to discard the peel. Mix all together, cover and leave to cool for at least 10 minutes. Beat the egg yolks well and add them to the mixture. Pour into a buttered oven-proof dish and bake for 40 minutes.

Meanwhile make the orange sauce by melting the marmalade gently in the orange juice. Cook to a pouring consistency but not too runny. Remove from heat, taste and add a dash of Cointreau.

Beat the egg whites until they form soft peaks. Add half the remaining sugar. Whip again, add the rest and beat again.

Remove the pudding from the oven and increase the temperature to 200C/Gas 6. Spread the pudding with the orange and Cointreau sauce then smooth on the meringue topping. Return to the oven for 5-8 minutes until the top is slightly browned. Leave to cool for 10 minutes or so before serving.

(*See My Store Cupboard Favourites, p.232)

Fromage Fort

This is a useful way of using up bits of cheese; spread onto slices of toasted stale baguette it's a tasty addition to serve with a lunchtime bowl of soup, and a good partner to a robust glass of red wine. A dish of fromage fort, some crusty bread, a bowl of fat black olives and a bottle of the aforementioned red is a perfect welcome to any friends who might drop by.

230g cheese bits including 'blue'
50g unsalted butter, softened
50g cream cheese
¼ cup dry white wine
1 garlic clove, peeled, crushed and creamed
freshly ground black pepper
a pinch of cayenne pepper
chopped chives and parsley

In a food processor, process the cheese and all other ingredients until smooth.

If necessary add more cream cheese to get good spreading consistency.

That's it really though you can play about with quantities and types of cheese.

You can freeze it too!

Pears with Roquefort

What could be simpler? This is something that I often serve as a cheese-cum-dessert course at the end of a simple meal. As always the fruit must be perfect and pears can be a little tricky. I like Williams pears best though they are not the greatest of keepers. If you are serving this outside of the season when pears are being harvested and ripened, then I find the Conference pear the most consistently reliable for sweetness, juiciness and texture.

Mash the Roquefort with some pouring cream, leaving it a little lumpy. Core the pears and divide into eight slices. Serve one pear per person, fanning out the slices on a plate and spooning over some of the Roquefort sauce. Scatter with a little chopped chervil.

CHAPTER 6

Reems, Rimes or Rance

We spent Bastille Day at Berry-au-Bac, a small village at the junction of the canal Latéral à l'Aisne and the canal de l'Aisne à la Marne. And indeed the day before that as well. Should you ever have passed through Berry you might wonder why anyone would choose to celebrate France's greatest historic event in such a godforsaken place. Mere circumstance is the answer. Namely an unscheduled stoppage for work on the lock the day before Bastille Day, then on the day itself the whole canal is closed. So now we must spend two days in the middle of nowhere with not a lot to do. In fact it's no bad thing just pottering about, doing a bit of towpath foraging, rubbing down and retouching the paintwork where we've embarrassed ourselves scraping along the wall when entering a lock, and having the time to discover a bit more about where we are.

Not so very long ago Berry-au-Bac was one of the places where working boats gathered and awaited their orders for freight. The chances of finding anywhere to tie up here almost nil and if you were lucky enough to squeeze into a space between the ranks of moored barges you treated your neighbours with deferential respect, grateful for even the merest nod of recognition. Now they've all gone and, although it may seem perverse, I am saddened that nowadays there's always plenty of room for the likes of us. We claim a spot immediately below the out-of-action lock, and at least when it re-opens we shall be the first through. Captain raises the mast – an indication to others that we are not going anywhere – and we try to decide what to do. Once when there were so many barges stopping here, a bar and *épicerie* close to the lock catered for all one's basic needs. It's closed now, as is the supplier of fuel and bottled gas – even the water tap has gone. At least there is a *boulangerie* in the village we tell each other and all the others who are steadily arriving and joining the queue – a German cruiser, a Danish yacht and a little Belgian owned tjalk. We all straggle off along the dusty main street to the baker's, only to discover they are closed and on their hols; we all straggle back again, hot, breadless and cross.

So what else does Berry-au-Bac have to offer that will keep us amused and out of trouble for two days? Well, believe it or not, there is a one star Michelin restaurant here, famously named 'Côte 108'. This in memory of the nearby crest of land over which the longest and bloodiest battles were fought during the First World War. Here, on 14 April 1917, the French army sustained its highest single casualty rate of the war: 40,000 men in one dreadful day. Even after all this time it is still possible to find, in the undergrowth, the telltale signs of old battles fought. And more poignantly, their consequence, as the thousands of graves in the nearby military cemeteries of both allies and enemy testify. Had I known more about the history of Berry when we first ate at Côte 108 I might not have enjoyed my meal quite so much.

We cheered ourselves up, Jeffrey Archer style, by drinking champagne with the last of the lamb, now making its final appearance at the table in the guise of shepherd's pie followed by the best rice pudding in the world.

Only one more day and we can go.

Reims is only a very short days boating from Berry-au-Bac. The French pronounce its name with a rolling rrrr and the word sort of rhymes with 'pants'. We British call it 'Reems' and the Americans say 'Rimes'. I guess we all know where we are talking about, though the French never seem to quite appreciate our efforts to say it their way. If asked by a lock-keeper where we are going we find it best to avoid saying it altogether; it is easier to proffer 'Paree' in response – then everyone is happy. We had arranged to meet friends and had finally booked an oft promised meal at the Brasserie du Boulingrin, so were determined to get there on time. First in the queue meant we were first away through the lock when it re-opened for business. The rest must now wait for *Edouard*, a loaded barge, which had been waiting to come down through the lock, before they could leave. We wished him *'bonne route'* as we passed and the same to the families on the other three laden craft, who had also been held up above the lock, as we slid by them.

A few hours later arriving below the first lock at Reims we could see that our friends were already there. We pulled into a space just ahead of their barge. We had booked a table for a late-ish dinner at the Boulingrin. It is a brisk walk from the canal, up through the town, past the cathedral and on towards the Avenue du Champagne – home to some of the greatest champagne houses. The restaurant is just opposite the Les Halles covered market which is undergoing a facelift, and a shift upmarket, with many of the more traditional marketeers displaced by the newer trendier fast-food outlets and elegant delis. Sad but surely a sign of the times; even in France the city-dwellers have less time for the older, slower ways. The Boulingrin stands out against such modernist trends. It has been going since 1925 and the vast dining room still retains its original art deco style. Although large, noisy and very busy, everything operates like clockwork. The staff are young, bright and efficient; in this sort of place you have to be. I remember, many years ago, working for a time in an incredibly popular London steak house. With a dozen or so tables to wait on it was really hard to keep track of what stage of their meal each set of diners was at; to make sure that no request for rolls, wine or water was forgotten and to serve every table at the right sort of pace. We worked absurdly long hours and needed to always show a cheerful face no matter how rude or demanding the customer. Since that time I have always held good waiting in very high esteem. Brasserie staff are the very best and of course this being France where service is, by law, already included on the bill, they are not doing it merely in hopes of tips.

The food was not to be sneezed at either.

With empty bilges encouraging us to get on down to the river Marne as soon as possible we waved 'goodbye' to our friends and left the following day. My list is made and if we do everything on it, will keep us busy for a week or two. For champagnes we must go to Henri Goutorbe in Aÿ, to Diebolt-Vallois at Cramant and to try somewhere new – we think the house of Leclerc Briant in Épernay sounds interesting. No champagne shopping would be complete without calling on Madame Salvatori in rue Flodoard. There's a prize-winning maker of a most excellent boudin noir that we sampled in the village of Fleurie-la-Rivière at a *vide grenier*. We know he has a shop somewhere in Épernay; he needs tracking down. While we are over at Cramant I want to call in at Nelly Vatel's duck farm at nearby Gionges. She oversees the production of superb foie gras and is very kind to her ducks.

With all this in mind we think we might stay at Condé-sur-Marne, a village at the other end of the Canal de l'Aisne à la Marne, for a few weeks. It is close to the River Marne and the champagne town of Épernay; not a particularly exciting place in itself but convenient to moor for a while and fairly close to all the places I am aiming to call at. There is a baker at Condé and about three kilometres away at Aulnay-sur-Marne a good pick-your-own fruit and vegetable grower who has a small but excellent farm shop. Here one can buy freshly pressed apple juice, new-laid eggs, free-range chicken and guinea fowl. A lot of boats pass through

Condé and, therefore, any number of people we are likely to know, so it's as well to be prepared for a bit of friendly champagne tasting and impromptu meals *'sur l'herbe'*.

First on the list on our arrival at Condé is to pop across the road to say *'bonjour'* to Madame Potié and purchase a bottle or two of her very reasonably priced Champagne Brut Ordinaire. This is not, by any means, the greatest champagne in the world but is more than good enough for everyday drinking and makes a fair Kir royale. I also wanted some of their delicious ratafia to fill the hollowed-out centres of the two small charentais melons I had planned as part of our meal that evening.

Though sometimes hard for us foreigners to get used to (but always remembering that Chauvin was a Frenchman) the French tend to eat and drink what's nearest, first. After that they may venture further afield, but rarely, culinarily speaking, far outside of France. I have come to regard this as a very civilised way of going on. (Except, of course, when desperate for a decent curry.) Our own more eclectic lifestyle permits a familiarity with a huge variety of wines from all over the world. We often know far more about the wines of the different regions of France than do the French themselves. They mostly stick to their local brew, and if this is Champagne then that's what they drink. Initially it was disconcerting to see diners in restaurants supping bubbly right through their meal. But it's what they do. Now we've tried it too and have found any number of robust champagnes that work reasonably well with a whole range of foods including, oddly, both veal and lamb.

Down at the fruit farm the strawberries are ready. They are grown in waist-high troughs and with no kneeling or bending involved it is so easy to pick way too many – which of course I do. We'll have strawberry soup. That will use up loads. Obviously I'll have to make some more Eton Mess; that will be this afternoon's treat to be taken on the stern deck with a glass of champagne perked up with a dash of crème de fraise. We move on to the unruly drifts of little yellow courgettes and the French bean bushes. Innate greediness pushes me on and again I pick more than we really need, though my equally strong mean streak will prevent my wasting too much and thus will hopefully result in some creative ways of using up the excess. In the shop I spot a plump-breasted duck. That's easily two good meals there. I'll roast it, courgettes baked with cream and mint will make a good accompaniment; any leftovers I'll turn into a duck pilau which we'll have with a helping of coconut cream and tomato curry. Leftover skin and bones will make a rich stock for soup or gravy. In the shop I round off the shopping with a bunch of fat spring onions, some fiery little radishes and a bottle of fresh apple juice. I mention my 'duck for dinner' thoughts to Captain. It's only fair to give him time to decide on the wine we'll drink with it and embark on a protracted search for the bottle in the bilges.

Early evening and it is very quiet at Condé, so quiet that as we sit in *Friesland's* wheelhouse, a sound – the merest of sighs – makes us look round. The sigh is followed by a sharp crack. In the apple orchard just a few yards from where we are moored a tree loaded down with fruit finally gives up the struggle to support the weight. We watch with shocked surprise as a whole branch splits away from the tree and falls to the ground. It happens so slowly and, apart from that initial sigh and crack, silently. What a melancholic moment; so sad that the tree's very fecundity should cause its demise. A fence separates us from the orchard and it is not possible to collect the apples. Next day the owner came and cleared everything up and that was that.

RECIPES

A Kir Royale

Loved by all – this is the 'go to' apéro. Traditionally Kir (named after the clever onetime mayor of Dijon) is a mix of blackcurrant liqueur and the wine made from the aligoté grape. This grape is indigenous to Burgundy and was, before the rise of chardonnay, the normal quaffing wine of the region. It used to be a particularly sharp and sour beverage, which made it almost unsaleable to anyone from outside of the area. Burgundy happens to be, happily, also a place where blackcurrants are grown in profusion. Here the crop is turned into the richly fruity liqueur known as Crème de Cassis. It was Mayor Kir's brilliant idea of adding a drop of the cassis to a glass of the acidic aligoté – *et voilà* – he turned it into the hugely popular apéritif it is today. And as a result greatly improved the fortunes of both the fruit and vine farmers within the region. Kir royale is made with champagne. Sadly, like so many other truly wonderful innovations, this simple drink can be brought low and turned into a travesty of itself by the unscrupulous or uncaring. Taste the sickly sweet, almost lukewarm concoction that is often palmed off on the unsuspecting tourist and you will get my drift. The secret to making a decent Kir is to always use the dry and flinty (and nowadays much improved) aligoté wine served very cold to which is added a mere dash of the liqueur. The same applies to the 'royale' made with champagne – choose the driest one you can find. As it happens they are usually the youngest and therefore the cheapest. To keep the sweetness under control, initially add the cassis incrementally and taste until you have the balance just right. Happily the firm of Védrenne based in Nuits St Georges in Burgundy makes a huge range of fruit liqueurs as well as the best quality Crème de Cassis. Not only can you ring the changes with this simple apéritif but a good dash of your chosen liqueur in a fruit dessert or jelly adds a certain *je ne sais quoi*-ness to the dish and keeps your guests tasting and guessing.

Strawberry Soup

Make no mistake – French strawberries in season are utterly delicious. In a pick-your-own situation, even after you've managed to eat three for every one you have put in your basket, it still takes quite a while to get to that 'oh no, not another strawberry' stage. I'm not a great lover of jam but the no-cook freezer jam I make is so freshly fruity that it lends itself to a whole raft of things to do with it. As for the soup, it's so simple to make, uses up a great many strawbs and is quite impressive if you have guests. Make sure it's really cold. Pour it into a big bowl and place in the middle of the table with a ladle and let everyone help themselves. Offer crème fraîche and almond tuiles.

For four
*   1 kilo of strawberries.*
Set to one side about a dozen or more of the best and hull the rest. Place them in a saucepan and squash them down a bit with a potato masher. Add about 100g of caster sugar and a drop of water. Bring the strawberries to simmering point, then add a small wineglassful of fruity red wine – a pinot noir as we are in champagne country – mixed with a flattened teaspoon of cornflour. Simmer for around 10 minutes. Leave to cool a little then liquidise. Pass through a fine sieve to get rid of all the pips. Pour into a bowl and stir occasionally while it cools down.

Up to here this is more or less the recipe in *Jane Grigson's Fruit Book*.

When the soup is cold I add a generous slug of Védrenne Crème de Fraise and a squeeze or two of lemon juice. Check for sweetness. If it is too thick, add a little more wine or water.

Plop the saved strawberries on the top. The soup should be just thick enough to stop them sinking out of sight. If you have it, a sprig of fresh mint placed in the centre of the soup gives that finishing touch.

Roast Duck

Duck is so tasty. Yes it is very fatty, but it is the fat that helps to give it its rich succulence and flavour. In any case you don't have to eat the fat as it virtually all drains out during the cooking process. The Chinese way of preparing a duck for roasting produces a wonderfully crisp dry skin. Try to do it like this if you have the time and think of it soon enough, but it is not the end of the world if you just prick the duck all over with a fork and shove it into the oven (yes, yes, duck not fork!).

1 duck, around 1.5 kg
salt and pepper

Prick the skin (not the flesh) all over with a sharp skewer, toothpick or similar. Place the duck on some sort of rack that you have put in the sink or over the top of a good-sized washing-up bowl. Pour a kettle or two of boiling water all over the duck. Allow it to dry on the rack, preferably near an open window or remove to the fridge and leave uncovered. This needs to be planned the day before so that your duck can dry overnight.

Preheat the oven to 230C/Gas 8.

Rub salt all over the dry skin and scatter some inside as well. Grind some black pepper inside too. Rest the duck on its wire rack on top of a large roasting pan and place in the centre of the oven. Roast for 20-30 minutes then turn the heat down to 180C/Gas 4. Roast for a further hour or more. Pour out the accumulated fat from the roasting dish into a bowl and use to sauté potatoes. Once the duck is cooked, remove from the oven, cover with a clean tea towel and sheet of foil and rest for about 20 minutes.

While the duck is resting cook the following recipe and sauté a few spuds.

Courgettes, Mint and Cream

For two

> *30g butter*
> *1 small clove of garlic, crushed*
> *250g freshly picked green or yellow courgettes the size of a fat finger*
> *approx 110ml whipping cream*
> *approx 50ml rich chicken or vegetable stock – made with a cube will do*
> *1 tablespoon mint, finely chopped*
> *Maldon sea salt and freshly ground white pepper*

Melt the butter in a wide low-sided pan. Add the crushed garlic and cook very gently in the butter. Do not let the garlic colour. Cut each courgette into chunky slices and add all to the pan. Stir round until well covered with the butter. Cook gently with lid on for a couple of minutes, then pour in a drop of the stock. Replace lid and cook for a further 3-5 minutes until the courgettes are just cooked but still with plenty of bite. Remove lid and cook off juices until you are left with just the buttery courgettes.

Fish out the crushed clove of garlic. Now pour in some cream – you may not need all of it – and add a little stock. Reduce it until it has the body of a pouring sauce. Stir in enough mint to flavour; too much will overpower the delicate courgettes. Leave to simmer gently for a moment or two. Taste and add seasoning if necessary.

On two hot plates serve slices of duck breast and some crispy skin. Spoon on the courgettes and pour the sauce over them both. Serve with crispy sautéed potatoes cooked in the duck fat. Finish with a light sprinkling of finely chopped fresh mint.

My Shepherd's Pie

I like this just as I remember it as a child, made with leftover lamb and dried mixed herbs and plenty of mash on top. We used to have it with tinned peas then but now I'm grown up I prefer to use fresh or frozen instead but that's the limit to my refinement.

For two

> *oil for frying*
> *100g of bacon, chopped*
> *a medium onion, chopped*
> *a medium carrot, chopped*
> *a stick of celery, chopped*
> *200g - 250g cooked lamb, chopped*
> *stock made with a lamb stock cube*
> *½ teaspoon of dried mixed herbs*
> *500g potatoes*
> *A little milk and butter*
> *Maldon sea salt and freshly ground pepper*
> *1 tablespoon parsley, finely chopped*

Heat a little oil in a shallow pan with a lid. Fry the bacon bits just to release the fat, add the chopped onion, carrot and celery and sweat all together for a few minutes. Add the lamb. Pour over enough lamb stock to cover and throw in the dried mixed herbs. Cover with a lid and leave to simmer on a low heat for about 20 minutes.

In the meantime boil and then mash the potatoes adding a drop of milk, a knob of butter, salt and pepper.

Pour the lamb mixture into a sieve set over a bowl to catch the gravy. Save the gravy. Taste the lamb and season with salt and pepper if necessary. Empty the lamb mixture into a baking dish just large enough to take the meat with the mash on top. Moisten it slightly with a little of the gravy and then pile on the potato.

If eating straight away dot the potato liberally with butter and spread around using the tines of a fork. Slide under a hot grill to allow the surface to brown and crisp up a little.

If intending to serve later finish the potato with the butter, cover with clingfilm and refrigerate until needed.

Preheat oven to 200C/Gas 6

Remove clingfilm and place in the centre of the oven. Allow about 20 minutes to heat through. If the top hasn't browned enough finish it off under the grill.

Check the gravy. If necessary add a little more crumbled stock cube, salt and pepper. Reheat when the Shepherd's Pie is ready to serve. Pile onto two warmed plates and scatter with the parsley. Pour on the gravy. You can, of course, serve almost any green vegetable with this on the side.

My Rice Pud

This has to be the best rice pudding you are ever going to eat. It is rich and creamy but at the same time light and airy. I know I call it *my* rice pud but truth to tell we first ate this very unlikely French dessert at restaurant 'Chez Michel' near the Gare du Nord in Paris; I spent years trying to replicate it. This recipe is, however, the real McCoy. How do I know? Because I finally got the recipe from chef, Thierry Breton, himself. The raisins in Saba is my addition; I think they work perfectly as a tasty topping for the rice.

For four

125g large golden raisins

6 tablespoons Saba

100g round pudding rice

500ml full-cream milk

vanilla pod cut in two down its length

125ml whipping cream

50g caster sugar

Put the raisins in a bowl and pour over just enough boiling water to cover. Leave to soak for 30 minutes, drain off any excess water and pour on the Saba. (Saba is a deliciously thick, simultaneously tart and sweet Italian grape syrup). Turn the raisins in this and leave to soak.

In a saucepan gently cook the rice in the milk, with the vanilla pod, until all the milk has been absorbed. Stir frequently and keep a sharp eye on it particularly towards the end when it wants to stick. At this point, as the last of the milk is absorbed, the whole thing looks a bit of a heavy, solid, mess. Leave it to cool.

Remove the vanilla pod. (Wash and dry it and use it to flavour a jar of caster sugar). In another bowl whip the cream adding the sugar little by little tasting as you go. If topping with something like the Saba soaked raisins it pays not to make the rice too sweet. Fold the cream gently into the rice. The stodgy mess will loosen and begin to look much more attractive.

Refrigerate and serve cold in pretty glass goblets with the raisins and Saba syrup drizzled over the top.

CHAPTER 7

A Forage Along the Towpath

Stopping at Condé-sur-Marne for a time allowed us to reacquire our 'shore' legs and also spend a while exploring the immediate vicinity. I do have the foraging bug and armed with my basket, a small pair of scissors and short, sharp knife, like nothing better than to search out and identify those bits of vegetation which might add some interest to our daily diet.

When we first started boating in France I thought the people I occasionally saw wandering along the towpath, peering into the undergrowth, were probably collecting greens for their rabbits. That's what we used to do as kids in England, and for city children like me, finding bunny food on bits of bombed-out wasteland was the nearest we ever got to foraging in the countryside. I soon discovered that anyone in France dawdling slowly along, basket in hand, nose to the ground, is likely to be after far richer pickings than a few dandelions for their pets.

After rain, in some regions, people still go out and gather snails. I've always considered this a problematic activity when you live on a boat. If they escaped and took to the bilges you'd probably be lumbered, before you knew it, with your own, albeit somewhat inaccessible, snail farm. I once saw live snails for sale in a French supermarket; home was a box on the fish counter where they were wandering about. Every so often the fish person collected them all up and put them back in their box. I was utterly delighted at the very notion of snails in a supermarket and watched their wanderings enthralled until 'looks' from the fish person made me move on. I've never gathered them after rain or in a supermarket either but I have bought them ready prepared for eating from a snail farm. I love snails and if you spend any time in France you really cannot avoid trying the famous delicacy and there are many more ways to eat them than just the eponymous snails in garlic butter. Although I really do enjoy them cooked that way.

However, thoughts on snails are for another time – this is about foraged food. And while we are, or were, on the subject of green things, there are several other good plants to look out for, apart from young nettle and dandelion leaves – both of which, in my opinion, are somewhat overrated as food for humans. Sorrel is a favourite and as we boat along a canal I always keep an eye on the towpath, looking out for its feathery pinky-brown seed heads. These give the game away as they wave around above the little leaves clustered at the base of the main stalk. Sorrel, whatever the variety, wild or cultivated, always has two little pointed ends at the bottom of each leaf and a sharp acidic taste. Two or three good handfuls will add a delicious lemony flavour to a cold cucumber or courgette soup. I make an instant sauce of melted butter and fine chopped sorrel to go with grilled salmon or mackerel; the sharpness of the sorrel cutting across the oiliness of the fish.

Wild asparagus is also easily identifiable from the boat. Its green fronds stand high and immediately attract attention as they shimmer in response to the gentlest of breezes. I've never seen it growing north of Paris but that may just be happenstance. Certainly it can be found in abundant patches alongside many canals. I have picked large bunches on the Canal du Loing and along lock cuts on the River Yonne. The season is short, about the same as for the domestic variety, so don't bother to look for it much after the end of May; too late – you will have missed it. But if you haven't, collect armfuls and cook it quickly in butter; if you've only managed to find a small amount, mix it with other spring vegetables, peas, broad beans, young carrots and baby turnips. It's delicious with anything fishy, in omelettes and as an ingredient in a creamy egg cocotte.

Rocket grows anywhere; I've even picked it on a roundabout in the middle of a very busy road junction. The towpath through Reims is full of it and it loves rough ground. You will find rocket growing happily on the little wastelands around the wharves and silos you find beside waterways. When we stop somewhere like this for the night, it is always worth going off for a bit of a forage before apéro time. Although difficult to distinguish at a distance from rape, up close the leaves identify it as rocket straight away. They have narrow-toothed lobes, hard to describe, though a little like the leaves of the oak tree, but once you have seen them you will always recognise them. I say: if in doubt taste it; the wild variety of rocket is particularly peppery, good in salads or wilted in butter and mixed with pasta or slices of polenta. Or like watercress, which can often be found in the fast-flowing water of small streams and ditches, is delicious piled high between two slices of fresh buttered bread with or without a smear of Marmite. Remember though, when you pick watercress in the wild, to wash it really well under running water before you eat it.

In spring I look out for wild garlic. You might be persuaded to pick it just for its prettiness but the strong smell of garlic makes it somewhat unsuitable in a vase of wild flowers. Never mind, it's that garlic-y brashness that you are after. Finely chopped in strips, it perks up a salad no end and preserved in jars with olive oil and a little salt, it can be used in all manner of ways. Wild garlic thrives in the sort of damp shady places found beside small rivers and streams.

Another of the wild greens and one of my all-time favourites is purslane. In France it appears almost anywhere once the weather is warm. It grows like a weed in Burgundy and I have no doubt everywhere else. The wild variety that I find near the canal adds a crunch of acidic sharpness to a green salad and just like the wild asparagus is delicious as a vegetable garnish for all sorts of dishes.

Elderflowers are a delight though I've still never managed to make a really successful cordial. It is difficult to get the balance perfectly right between the scent of the delicate blossom, a lemony sharpness and some sweetness. One does keep trying though as elders are endemic to towpaths. I do however make great elderflower and champagne jellies which look so alluring with the tiny fresh flowers trailed across the surface. Elderberries too, hugely tart, make a good country wine, though definitely needing to be kept a couple of years or more before it is fit to drink. There is always a bottle or two stashed away with the sloe gin in *Friesland's* deep bilges.

During early Summer you can often find tiny strawberries hidden away in the undergrowth at the edges of the towpath. They are not always that exciting I have to say; a lot of pips for their size and I rarely come across too many of them. If I do manage to find a small handful of really ripe ones I drop two or three into the bottom of a champagne glass, add a drop of crème de fraise and top up with some very dry sparkling wine. As with a Kir royale (traditionally champagne and crème de cassis), the more sharply acidic the champagne, the better the balance with the sweet intensity of the fruity alcoholic juice.

Which brings me nicely on to cherries and Napoleon. I sometimes wonder just how many of the benevolent actions ascribed to old Boney are actually true. Nevertheless I do have it on good authority that, as with the passing of the bread laws and the planting of plane trees, so it is with the fruit and nut trees that are found growing along all the canal routes of France. He decreed that several different types should be planted. Most quoted are apples and pears, cherries and plums, hazel and walnuts, though in the south I've seen apricots and peaches too. This was done to ensure a ready supply of collectable food for all the families who worked and travelled along the waterways. I do hope it is true. It is certainly a fact that all these trees can still be found in some abundance on most canals.

In the early days when we were first boating in France I asked a lock-keeper if I might pick up the windfalls littering the towpath. He gave me a quizzical look and asked me why I would want to eat squashed and wormy apples off the ground when they were so much better picked straight from the tree? I've never looked back. The best pears in red wine we ever had were small and rock hard and came from a half dead tree on the Aisne à la Marne canal. On the Briare canal I've collected and bottled the sour little cherries known as *griottines* which even the birds won't touch, and used them, once they have been slowly marinated in sugar and alcohol, in the same way as the wild strawberries. The bonus is that the alcohol they are bottled in becomes deeply cherry flavoured over time and is very drinkable on its own; good in a trifle too.

And just don't get me started on walnuts, which grow everywhere along the waterways. Well do (get me started), as they enjoy a double season; once in July and again in September. Collect them in midsummer when they are still soft and green and before the hard casing has formed and you can pickle them. Delicious served in the traditional way with a crumbly Cheshire or mature Cheddar, pickled walnuts also introduce an interestingly elusive flavour when a few are chopped small and added to a beef stew or a lentil salad. Even better is the splendid walnut liqueur found in every French country woman's wine cellar, maturing away, to be ready for the Christmas after next. Make it from a handful of the green immature nuts – there's really nothing to it. Later in the year, at the end of September, early October, is the time to take a stroll along almost any towpath in France and you will find more walnuts than you think you could ever want or know what to do with. Trust me, collect lots and you will find so many uses for them.

As the cooler weather approaches one's thoughts naturally turn towards the mushroom. Parasols and shaggy ink-caps often grow slap-bang in the middle of the towpath, horse mushrooms suddenly appear in the fields beside it, and the occasional pure white puffball can turn up under a hedge. It pays to keep your eyes peeled and the binoculars to hand.

On this occasion I found an abundance of sorrel and rocket, collected some wild marjoram and mint, and picked a huge number of golden dandelion flower heads to transform into a delicious jelly preserve. Watercress too, that came from a small feeder stream to the Marne; the picking proved somewhat perilous and I ended up soaking wet, but triumphant.

RECIPES

Cold Sorrel and Cucumber Soup

This is a lovely tangy soup. It's an ideal starter to a light meal, maybe followed by a simple quiche and salad, with fresh fruit to finish. Young courgettes can be used instead of cucumber. The original recipe came from Lindsey Bareham's book, *A Celebration of Soup*. Using the sorrel raw at the end of the cooking is an idea from Margaret Costa's *Four Seasons Cookery Book*. The flavour is fresher and the sorrel less of a sludgy colour.

For six

> 6-8 *spring onions, chopped*
>
> 1 *tablespoon unflavoured oil (I like to use grapeseed)*
>
> 2 *cucumbers, peeled, de-seeded if necessary and chopped*
>
> *a good handful of sorrel leaves, any thick stalks removed, the leaves washed and*
> *sliced into fine strips*
>
> *chicken or vegetable stock to cover (unless I actually have some well flavoured and*
> *degreased home-made chicken stock I tend to use Knorr liquid chicken stock or*
> *Marigold vegetable bouillon powder*)*
>
> 275 *ml of pouring cream*

Sweat the onion in the oil for a couple of minutes before adding the
cucumber. Gently cook both together for a further 5 minutes. Pour over
just enough stock to cover. Bring to the boil, then turn the heat down to a
gentle simmer and cook for about 30 minutes. Once the cucumber is soft,
allow to cool, then process in two or three batches adding the raw sorrel
leaves to each batch and reduce to a smooth cream. Add the cream and
more cold stock if you think it needs thinning down. Check and adjust the
seasoning after adding any extra stock as this will already be salty. Finish
with a scattering of finely chopped narrow strips of sorrel.

(*See My Store Cupboard Favourites, pp. 234, 237)

Wild Asparagus with Scrambled Eggs and Smoked Salmon

You will need a big bunch of wild asparagus. For this dish I use just the
little tips and about 5cm of stalk. The rest can be kept to make an
asparagus puree to use as a base for another cold soup. This dish makes a
great Sunday brunch, particularly if you have friends staying with you.
Select your mooring spot where you know the asparagus can be found and

send your guests off the following morning to find and pick. Hopefully they will eventually return triumphant and you, with a bit of luck, will have had a couple of hours peace and quiet. Drink champagne with the brunch. If you are unable to collect the wild, this dish can also be made with shop bought asparagus sprue.

For four

> *2 handfuls of asparagus tips*
> *Maldon salt and freshly ground black pepper*
> *100g butter*
> *4-6 slices of smoked salmon*
> *10 fresh eggs,*
> *2 tablespoons cream*
> *2 tablespoons chives, cut into short lengths*

Blanch the asparagus tips in boiling salted water for no more than 60 seconds. Drain, cool and dry on kitchen roll. Melt 25g of butter in a small pan. Once it is melted have the asparagus at hand ready to drop into the pan to reheat and finish cooking. Do not do this until the scrambled eggs are virtually cooked.

Tear the smoked salmon into rough pieces.

Melt the remaining 75g butter in a shallow heavy-based pan on the lowest possible heat you can arrange. Break the eggs into a bowl and beat lightly with a fork. Tip into the pan with the hot, melted butter and stir. Cook over a low heat, stirring more or less continually with a wooded spatula. It can take about 5 minutes for the eggs to be just set and become very creamy. If you prefer a firmer finish, cook for a minute or two longer.

Add the cream, the chives and the warm buttery asparagus. Stir gently and add the salmon pieces. They will just begin to lightly cook in the hot egg mixture.

Serve immediately on warm plates with slices of toasted malty brown loaf or even some dark German rye bread.

Puffballs in Breadcrumbs

These are a rare treat. I have only ever found one near a towpath though I was once lucky enough to catch a beautifully fresh one that some kids threw at the boat as we passed by. I have occasionally bought them in a country market at the right time of the year. They can be quite big and are pure white right the way through; they should only be used when very fresh and are perfect with bacon and eggs for an indulgent weekend breakfast.

For two or three
> *50g butter, possibly more*
> *1 tablespoon olive oil, possibly more*
> *a garlic clove flattened, but not chopped*
> *salt and pepper*
> *slices of puffball about 5mm thick*
> *1 egg, lightly beaten and poured onto a dinner plate*
> *3 or 4 slices of fresh bread turned into finely ground breadcrumbs, spread out on another dinner plate*
> *eggs and bacon to serve*

Preheat oven to 170C/Gas 3

Heat the butter and oil with the garlic in a frying pan until a breadcrumb crisps when dropped in. Remove the garlic before it browns and discard.

Salt and pepper the puffball slices, then turn them first in the beaten egg and then in the breadcrumbs.

Fry gently on each side until crisp and golden. As you cook the puffball slices you may need to add more oil and butter to the pan, so make sure it is properly hot before putting in the next batch.

Once the slices are cooked, slide them onto a heated dish and place in a warm oven while you fry some eggs and grill the bacon. Place two slices of puffball to a plate each topped with a fried egg. Arrange the bacon around the eggs. Serve immediately.

Alternatively, forget the eggs and bacon and try it with this salsa.

Tomato, Avocado and Cucumber Salsa

For two

>   *1 large ripe avocado, peeled and stone removed,*
>   *2-3 ripe plum tomatoes, skins removed*
>   *½ fresh ridge cucumber, peeled*
>   *½ red onion, thinly sliced*
>   *2 tablespoons coriander, chopped*
>   *1 garlic clove creamed with a little sea salt*
>   *juice ½ a lime*
>   *1 tablespoon sweet chilli sauce*

First make the salsa by chopping the first 4 ingredients into same size chunky bits. Mix them all together in a bowl with the coriander. In another small bowl make the dressing by mixing the garlic, lime juice and chilli sauce together. Taste for balance. Pour over the salsa ingredients and turn them gently in the dressing.

Once all the puffball slices are cooked, remove from oven and serve a couple of slices per person on warm plates with the salsa on the side. Finish with a scattering of chopped coriander.

Sorrel Risotto

Sorrel has a fresh citrus tang that marries well with Parmesan cheese. A similar version to mine used to be one of the most popular dishes at Gennarro Contaldo's restaurant Passione, and with good reason.

For four
>*1.5 litres light chicken stock*
>*2 tablespoons olive oil*
>*a small knob butter, about 25g*
>*1 small white onion, finely chopped*
>*1 celery stalk, finely chopped*
>*375g Italian risotto rice*
>*150g well-rinsed sorrel, stalks removed and the leaves roughly chopped*
>*150g butter*
>*50g Parmesan cheese, freshly grated*
>*sea salt and freshly ground black pepper*

Bring the chicken stock (which you can make with Knorr Concentrated Chicken* stock) to a gentle simmer and leave on a low heat.

Gently heat the olive oil and knob of butter in a medium sized heavy-based pan – a Le Creuset casserole is ideal. Add the onion and celery and sweat without colouring until soft. Add the rice, stir well to ensure every grain has a coating of oil and the rice becomes shiny. Add a ladle or two of stock and cook, stirring all the time, until it has been absorbed. Continue adding the stock in this way until the rice is cooked.

This takes about 20 minutes or more. It is done when the rice tastes soft on the outside but is still a little al dente inside.

Remove from the heat, add the sorrel, butter and cheese. The sorrel will immediately wilt, turning a sludgy green, in the heat of the risotto. Beat well with a wooden spoon to obtain a creamy consistency. Taste and adjust seasoning. Leave to rest for a minute or two before serving.

(*See My Store Cupboard Favourites, p.237)

Pickled Walnuts

The method for pickling walnuts has hardly changed over the centuries, only the choice of aromatics varies a little from recipe to recipe. Wear gloves.

> *Pick about 900g of green walnuts*
> *Make 1 litre of standard brine – 140g salt dissolved into 570ml water x 2.*

Leave the walnuts to soak in the brine for four or five days. Drain them and leave them in the sun for another couple of days to dry and blacken. Once blackened, pack them into dry sterilised jars to almost full.

Make 1 litre of pickling vinegar:
> *570ml wine vinegar*
> *170g light muscovado sugar*
> *2.5cm peeled fresh ginger*
> *6 cloves*
> *piece of mace or cinnamon*
> *6 cardamom pods*
> *12 whole allspice berries*
> *½ teaspoon coriander seeds*
> *½ teaspoon dill seeds*

Put 140ml vinegar with the sugar and spices into a stainless steel saucepan. Bring to the boil and simmer for 30 minutes. Stir in the rest of the vinegar and bring back to the boil.

Pour the boiling vinegar over the walnuts making sure that all the spices are evenly distributed throughout the jars. Cover and seal while still hot. Allow them to mature for at least a month before using. They will keep unopened for a year or two.

Walnut Liqueur

I have sometimes wondered if, in France, there is an official walnut picking Sunday. We pass dozens of the trees when we are boating. They are always loaded down with nuts and ne'er a soul to be seen anywhere near. Come the middle of September every single tree is stripped bare, seemingly in the course of just one day. Whole families, armed with lumps of wood to throw up into the trees in hopes of dislodging the nuts, arrive in their dozens. They pass like locusts leaving nothing behind other than walnut detritus: broken sticks, discarded shells and scattered leaves.

In fact, for this delicious *digèstif* the walnuts need to be green with their shells still soft – we usually pick them around the end of June.

25 green walnuts
1 litre eau de vie
7.5cm cinnamon stick
4 cloves
1 walnut leaf
600g of sugar

Use rubber gloves – walnuts stain your hands nicotine yellow which no amount of scrubbing will remove; the gloves not only give protection but will save you days of explanations.

Cut each walnut into 6 longitudinal wedges and put them in a large container with the eau de vie and spices.

NB. Do not add the sugar at this stage

Seal the jar and leave it in a sunny warm place for a couple of months, shaking it from time to time.

At the end of this period, strain the liquid through a fine sieve into a jug. Make the syrup with half the sugar and two tablespoons of water. Bring to the boil to melt the sugar. In another saucepan caramelise the remaining sugar. When just brown (don't let it burn) remove from the heat and gently pour in the boiling syrup, stirring all the time. Allow the syrup to cool, then mix it with the strained walnut liquid. Add the walnut leaf. Pour back into the jar, seal it and leave for a further six weeks, giving it a shake now and then. At the end of this period, filter the walnut liquid once more and pour it into sterilised bottles. Seal and age for at least a year, preferably two, if you can hold out that long, before broaching a bottle.

Dandelion Jelly Preserve

This is a recipe which I found in a fascinating cook-book about the life and food of a village in the Auvergne written by Peter Graham. An ideal recipe for someone with not a lot to do, as it requires the collection of a huge number of dandelion flower heads, and you do need to get up early to pick them. I was prompted to try it when we stopped for a few days close to a patch of land that was completely covered with them. I gave up after picking two hundred dandelions so only made half the amount, which was enough for us. It's definitely worth making though as it is really tasty, with a flavour hard to identify, and is supposedly good for soothing sore throats.

To make 2kg of jelly:

> *400 newly opened dandelion flowers*
> *2 oranges*
> *1 lemon*
> *1kg caster sugar*

Trim off all the green parts from the flowers so that only the yellow petals are left. Cut the oranges and lemons, unpeeled, into slices and throw into a large pan. Add the flowers and 2 litres of water. Bring to the boil and simmer for about an hour until half the water has evaporated. Strain the liquid into a bowl, pressing down to extract every drop. Put through a jelly bag into a new pan. Add the sugar, bring back to the boil, stirring all the time, and simmer gently for 45 minutes.

Test the jelly by dropping a small amount onto a cold plate. If it sets the jelly is ready, otherwise cook for a little longer. Allow to cool and pour into sterilised pots.

Wild Strawberry Royale

Not so much a recipe, more of a congratulatory glass for all that foraging and bottling. If you have managed to find some sweet wild strawberries then they will do very well, otherwise some tiny bought *fraise de bois* will be perfect too.

For four with a small top-up
> *crème de fraise**
> *2 or 3 wild strawberries per glass*
> *1 bottle of dry champagne (actually any dry fizzy wine will do)*

Simplicity itself. Drop the strawberries into champagne flutes. Add enough crème de fraise to cover them and top up with the wine. Taste, and if too tart, add a little more crème de fraise. Do it this way round and you will avoid making it too sweet.

You can use the bottled *griottines* (see Ch.8) in the same way except now you just need to add some of the alcohol that the *griottines* have been maturing in instead of the fruit crème. Top up with champagne.

The drier the champagne (or other sparkling wine) the better. It needs to be quite sharp in order to balance the sweetness of the other ingredients. In fact this may be the one time when a cheap acidic champagne is the best option.

(*See My Store Cupboard Favourites, p.239)

Sandwiches

Making of a sandwich hardly counts as a recipe but does serve as a reminder of how delicious are certain combinations of fillings, not just the tastes but textures too, when slapped between a couple of slices of good bread. These two I just love to eat when I have some freshly foraged greenstuffs.

> *Watercress and Marmite*
> *Rocket and Cream Cheese*

My favourite bread for making both these sandwiches is an ordinary mixed grain loaf. I prefer unsalted butter. Make sure the greens are well washed and dried, with any big stalks removed. The Marmite is optional but just a smear across the butter and then loads of watercress packed on top is so good. Place the second buttered slice on top and press down a little before slicing in two.

Likewise the sandwich made with rocket: butter the bread and cover with a generous layer of creamy cheese: a garlicky shop-bought Boursin, or young fresh goats' cheese, work equally well here. Just make sure that the rocket is crisp and not too 'stalky' and that there is plenty of it.

CHAPTER 8

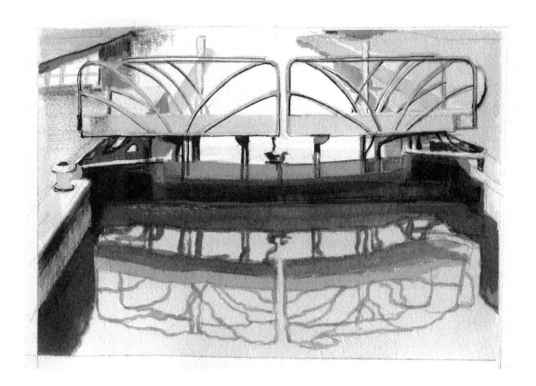

Afloat in Champagne

We are still at Condé-sur-Marne awaiting news on several possible canal closures due to water shortages. As so often happens, rain buckets down relentlessly night and day, rivers are rising all around and the possibility of drought seems laughable. Nevertheless 'those in charge' must deliberate and we must wait.

The weather has been gruesome. There have been no chance meetings with passing bargees, no ad hoc suppers beneath the trees, no popping of corks around the communal barbecue; indeed no barbecue, and thus none of the seasonal rituals we have come to so look forward to.

In the right company, semi-raw sausages, burnt steak and rough wine is fine – it's the next day the problems arise. But for the most part, this year, it has just been us.

We did, however, make some new friends last week-end. They are staying at a chambres d'hôtes just down the road in Tours-sur-Marne. They wanted to talk to us about their plans to buy a barge and so invited us to join them there for dinner. As it is now August which means that every restaurant for miles around is closed with owners on their month-long *congés annuels*, we accepted with alacrity.

The couple who run the place are charming; their ancient house and well-tended garden delightful. The owner, who is our host and tonight's chef, welcomes us to his home; he tells us that it was once the residence of a former boss of the champagne house of Laurent-Perrier, whose premises are just along the road.

He seats us at a long table in the conservatory and pours glasses of his cousin's blanc de blanc champagne made from chardonnay grapes from the other side of the Marne. He tells us that tonight he is cooking a simple meal using, in the main, only fruit and vegetables from his own garden. We sip our champagne and wait eagerly for the other group of guests who are staying there and who are to join us for dinner. It is a father with his two teenage daughters. They are from Bavaria in southern Germany. They speak excellent English and once my Captain has trotted out his best (and only) German phrase *'in der Nacht sind alle Katzen grau'* (Nietzsche) we gratefully revert to our mother tongue.

Our fellow guest asks us what we all do and we explain about *Friesland*; how when we are not bumbling around France Captain runs a barge-handling school. I tell him I have a 'foodie' blog and am in the process of writing a cook book. Our new friends regale him with their plans to run a hotel boat on the Seine which they want to operate as a cookery school. Hearing all this his eyes light up. He clearly has an interest in food. I ask him what he does and he says he is a chef and owns a restaurant in Germany.

The common interest is thus established.

We talk on, sharing our lives and experiences. Chunks of sweet Charentais melon are served which we dip into small glasses of the local ratafia before eating them, catching the drips on our tongues. Our patron arrives with a huge tureen of soup he has made using apples and courgettes from his garden. We are all getting along swimmingly. We ask about the restaurant and what sort of cooking our German does; he says they concentrate particularly on vegetables and local river fish with an emphasis on the produce of the region. I think 'nothing new there then' and say, rather archly, to Andree our new German friend, 'So are you working towards a Michelin star for your restaurant?'

He replies in his heavily accented English 'I heff to,' and we all nod sagely. My brain goes bleep … hang on … what did he just say? 'I have to', meaning that is what he feels he must do to make his restaurant a success, or, could he just possibly have said 'I have two'? In the silence that follows I ask him, 'Did you say you have two? Do you mean stars?' 'Yes,' he says in a shyly self-effacing sort of way.

There follows an even longer pause as we digest this bombshell at the same time as our next course of stuffed tomatoes and rice arrives. I realise that our patron probably has no idea that he is serving his simple home-cooked food to a two-star Michelin chef who might well have been expecting, as a visitor to France, a rather more sophisticated meal.

There is cheese from the region: Vignotte, Brie de Meaux and Langres, followed by a *tarte aux prunes*; I can see the tree from where we sit, still loaded down with plums. The chat is relaxed; we talk about the different champagnes we have tried and which ones we think the best. He describes the building in Nuremberg in which his own restaurant is housed; known as the Essigbrätlein, it is a place where food has been served for more than 500 years. Incredible.

I couldn't wait to get back to the boat to find out more. I google the name Andree Köthe and find various reviews of what is clearly a highly idiosyncratic form of cooking. The restaurant Essigbrätlein is in the heart of the old city. Gastronomically famous for its Bratwursts – a sausage which reflects its citizen's love of simple rustic food, what they make of this tiny culinary deviant in their midst is anyone's guess. Though 'Essigbrätlein' has the look of a typical Bavarian Gasthaus what it offers is a world away from unsophisticated peasant fare; thank goodness there is room enough for both.

The restaurant has two Michelin stars and eighteen Gault et Millau points awarded consistently since 2008. Surely this is a man with every right to brag a bit about his achievements. All I know is that we met a pleasant, thoughtful, unpretentious man on his holidays with his two girls

and that we sat around a table together, enjoying a simple meal in each others' company.

So much for the serendipidious nature of the barging life.

We decide that we really should get on and do our champagne shopping. Next day first call is to Henri Goutorbe in Aÿ. We love his pink champagne, it's gutsy, and works well with food. Already I am planning a highly indulgent meal of pasta with scallops and fennel to go with a Goutorbe Blanc de Noir. He is one of the rare growers who has older wines for sale, and at very reasonable prices. We two slightly shabby bargees sit in the foyer and taste them all – with gusto – talk about living the life of Riley!

It's time we tried someone new, although over the years we have probably drunk the very best that the smaller growers have to offer and the best-est best is Jacques Selosse at Avize. When I am rich, his will be the only champagne that will ever pass my lips. Sadly, nowadays, a case of six bottles of his 'Substance' sets one back a good few hundred euros even were you to try, as we do, sidling round to his back door for it. Should you manage to arrange a cellar visit, Anselme's (son of Jacques, now deceased) dedication, verve and originality are overwhelming and if he thinks you are interested in his obsession he will regale you with all the finer details of how he concocts his magnificent brew; it's a long and complicated process and an education to hear about.

Not so Francis Egly of Egly-Ouriet at Ambonnay who won't even let you over the threshold. You must give him your order through the barely open door and then wait outside. Legend has it that he will not even allow professional wine writers to use a spittoon as it shows disrespect for his wine. And the likes of us must take what he sells on trust because lowly you are not going to be allowed even the merest of sips before you buy. But his champagne is one of the truly greats, so worth the odd kick in the teeth (sort of) once one has plucked up the courage to ring his bell.

Another grower we rate very highly is the family of Diebolt-Vallois over at Cramant and who are rather more approachable than Mr Egly. Isabelle, daughter of the house, can only spare us twenty minutes. She rushes us across to the huge modern hangar that houses their stock of new oak barrels and stainless steel vats. No sign here of ill-lit musty cellars lined with dusty bottles. All is shiny clean and bright and she is a seriously hyperactive lady. Offering us a generous selection of their wines to taste she asks if we know the British company that is soon to import their champagne into the UK. Of course we do, though I dread to think what the cost of a bottle of Diebolt-Vallois Fleur de Passione would be, bought from the shop in St James Street in London; I can only be grateful that we can still just about afford to buy at source.

From Cramant, we head off to Nelly Vatel's duck farm at Gionges. I know it's all a bit non-pc nowadays to even mention foie gras, never mind admitting to liking and indeed to actually eating the stuff, so look away now if it's not your thing. My concession to conscience consists of trekking off to Nelly's whenever I can. I prefer to buy here rather than from shops where the provenance is unknown. At least at the farm you can see the ducks being fed, and, judging by the way they rush over with necks stretched forward and open beaks, they are not unduly concerned about being fed by *gavage*.

On Mondays when the farm shop and restaurant are closed one can call in at the kitchen and see how the foie gras is prepared. The local ladies employed by Nelly are very adept, quickly separating the lobes, removing all the yucky bits and then reshaping them. After that the foie gras is sprinkled with cognac, covered, refrigerated and later cooked. If you aim to have a go at cooking it yourself then it is useful to see at first-hand how it is prepared. Foie gras freezes well so I buy a couple of vacuum packed uncooked lobes for high days, holidays and any other time when we might fancy some. Two jars of mi-cuit pâté, some jars of duck confit and a pot of Nelly's really tasty onion marmalade adds up to quite a hefty bill but it will be several months before we eat them all, the cost therefore, spread over the whole period, is really very low. In fact, I have to agree with myself, it's quite a bargain.

Finally we have our day out in Épernay. We have arranged a tasting at Leclerc-Briant, intend to visit Madame Salvatori and to track down that prize-winning boudin noir maker. The degustation is arranged for 10.00 am. We climb the elegant staircase and are ushered into a very grand oak-panelled room. Tall windows look out over the town. The view is superb. Perched on spindly, somewhat fragile chairs and seated at a grand Louis XIV table, we feel, simultaneously, both genteel and scruffy − and fairly uncomfortable. Nevertheless, we manage to drink a glass of each of their champagnes and listen to an explanation of how they are made. All their wine has been produced biodynamically since the year 2000. An intriguing thought this! My dictionary defines the word as 'a method of organic farming involving such factors as the observation of lunar phrases and planetary cycles and the use of incantations and ritual substances'; fascinating and slightly mind-boggling stuff, eh? I have images of staid champagne farmers dancing naked among their rows of vines under a bright harvest moon, chanting incantations, and knocking back concoctions made from magic mushrooms. We buy three bottles of their La Ravinne 100% Pinot Meunier if for no other reason than to remind ourselves of the things that might go on in the dead of night up on the Montagne de Reims.

At Monsieur Colliaux's *charcuterie* I buy several of his famous blood sausages; he even throws in an extra one as a *cadeau*. I have an idea for making a stuffing of boudin noir and prunes to try with rabbit.

There's just time before the whole of France shuts up shop for the sacred lunch-time period to call in at Madame Salvatori's. She is now quite elderly and despite her name (she is the widow of a Sicilian gentleman), is very French and knows her champagnes. Yet this is essentially a grocer's shop that happens also to sell fine wines of the region. Only here can you join a queue, as we once did, clutching a bottle of the hugely expensive Philipponnat champagne, made exclusively from vines in the legendary walled enclosure known as the Clos des Goisses, and await our turn to pay behind a lad holding a bag of crisps and a can of Coke. Surely this must be the very essence of French *egalité*. Madame Salvatori has lists of every champagne she has for sale with the prices beside; one can leaf through these before buying. We sometimes consult her about which ones to buy but she always just answers with a faint smile, 'This wine is *"correct"*,' and it is hard to know whether she is handing out praise or damning the product. She makes us up a case of the six champagnes we have decided to try and then invites us to visit her house on the banks of the Marne on Sunday afternoon. Sadly we have to say no as we are leaving soon but hope she will remember to invite us again when we return next year.

With bilges well stocked and *Friesland* floating a little lower in the water, it is time to make tracks towards Burgundy – weather permitting.

RECIPES

Pâté en Croûte

Nowadays we are more used to pâtés which are cooked in earthenware terrines in enclosed ovens. Once such meat mixes were baked in open wood-fired ovens and so required a casing of pastry to retain their moisture. Pâté wrapped in pastry is still a popular dish in the Champagne region and one that is perfect for the itinerant boater. Available in most bakers and *charcuteries* it is easily very slightly warmed in the oven. Served with a green salad – lunch for the day is done.

I always think when I make something like this, it is what I call 'proper cooking'; it's immensely satisfying to do but will take up a good part of the day so clear the decks before you start.

These ones are a little like miniature pork pies. I think when there are just the two of us they are better, and stay fresher, than making one big one. They freeze well too so although the preparation and cooking takes time, you can make enough for several subsequent snacks, lunches or starters.

This recipe comes from Anne Willan's *French Regional Cooking.*

Makes about 20 small pâtés

 125g unsmoked bacon, diced

 125g veal escalopes, diced

 125g cooked ham, diced

 1 egg beaten with ½ teaspoon of salt (for the glaze)

Marinade

 2 tablespoons dry white wine

 2 tablespoons cognac

 2 tablespoons Madeira

 pinch of dried thyme

 1 bay leaf

 ½ yellow onion chopped

 2 teaspoons vegetable oil

Pâté pastry dough

 700g plain flour

 375g softened unsalted butter (or 1 part lard to 2 parts butter), softened

 2 eggs, separated

 2 tablespoons vegetable oil

 12g salt

 4-8 tablespoons cold water

Minced meat mixture:

 125g lean pork

 125g fat pork

 125g veal

 90g chicken livers

 2 tablespoons dry white wine

 1 tablespoon cognac

 1 egg

 1 teaspoon ground allspice

 sea salt and freshly ground black pepper

Place the diced bacon, pork and veal in a shallow dish. Mix all the marinade ingredients and add to the meat; mix well. Leave to marinate for 30-45 minutes.

Make the pastry by sifting the flour onto a work surface and making a large well in the centre. Put the softened butter (or lard/butter mix), the egg yolks, salt and most of the water into the well and work together with the fingertips of one hand until partly mixed. Draw the flour in steadily, pulling the dough together with both hands. If it feels a little dry, sprinkle with more water. The dough should be soft but not sticky. Work small portions of dough individually, pushing it away from you on the work surface, then gathering it up with a spatula. Keep working it until the dough is smooth and pliable. Gather it all together into one ball and chill for 30 minutes until firm.

For the meat mixture: mince (or process) together the lean and fat pork with the veal and chicken livers. Mix them in a bowl with the rest of the minced meat ingredients. Work it all with your fingers until it is an homogenous mass. Drain the diced meats from their marinade and mix them into the minced meat.

Sauté a very small amount of the mixture and taste for seasoning.

On a floured board roll out the pastry dough to a thickness of 6mm, then cut it into 12.5cm squares. In the centre of each square place a little oblong of the mix measuring about 4 x 7.5 cm – mound it up a little. From each corner of the pastry cut 1.25cm squares (like stamps). Brush the pastry around the meat with egg glaze and wrap the pâtés up like parcels. Turn them over and place them with seam side underneath on a prepared baking tray. Brush all over with the egg glaze.

Roll out the dough trimmings and decorate the tops of the pâtés with cut out leaves using the tip of a knife to mark the veins. Brush with the glaze. Make a small hole in the top of each with a sharp knife. Insert little tubes made out of tinfoil in the holes to allow any steam to escape.

Chill the pastries for 15 minutes.

Set the oven temperature to 200C/Gas 6 and bake them for 12-15 minutes or until they begin to brown. Lower the heat to 175C/Gas 4 and continue baking for a further 25-30 minutes or until a metal skewer inserted into the middle of a pâté for 30 seconds comes out hot to the touch. If they brown too quickly cover them loosely with tinfoil while they finish cooking.

Discard the little 'chimneys' and serve the pâtés warm with a lightly dressed green salad.

Scallops, Fennel and Pappardelle

Pappardelle comes from the verb 'pappare' which means 'to gobble up'. It is an egg-based dry pasta similar to tagliatelle but the ribbons are wider and more substantial. Although traditionally paired with rich sauces of wild boar or hare I think it works equally well with the scallops. Remember though that in this case you don't want to overwhelm the other ingredients with carbohydrate so be very sparing with the amount you serve.

For four
> *3-5 plump scallops with coral per person*
> *3 fresh fennel bulbs (save the fresh green leaves for the garnish)*
> *150g butter*
> *2 tablespoons Pernod (or similar)*
> *1 wine glass Noilly Prat* (or another light dry white wine)*
> *2 teaspoons concentrated chicken stock** or just under half a chicken stock cube*
> *75 ml water*
> *100g butter*
> *lemon juice*
> *enough pasta to put a few ribbons on each plate*

(*See My Store Cupboard Favourites, p.238, ** p.234)

Clean the scallops, remove the small hard muscle, and remove the corals. Chop each coral into three and put them in a separate bowl. Cover and refrigerate both until needed.

Take off any tough outer layers from the fennel. Slicing downwards, cut each bulb in half and then each half into three wedges. In a shallow-sided pan gently melt 50g of butter. Add the fennel and turn gently in the butter for a few minutes. Add 1 tablespoon of Pernod, turn up the heat a little and allow it to evaporate. Add the wine, the chicken stock and a little water. Bring to a gentle simmer then cover the pan with a (preferably see-through) lid and turning the fennel occasionally, allow it to cook until just al dente.

Once cooked, drain off the buttery juices into another pan and reheat. Keep the fennel warm while you complete the rest of the recipe. Add the rest of the Pernod and a little more chicken stock, if necessary, to the pan of juices to make up to about 140ml. Bring to the boil and reduce by about a quarter. Cut 100g of cold butter into small bits. Add two or three bits at a time and whisk in well. Make sure the sauce stays close to the boil and continue adding the butter until the sauce has thickened and has a bit of a sheen. Leave on a very, very low heat giving it a whisk now and again.

In the meantime cook the pappardelle according to the instructions on the packet. Drain and leave it to sit in a drop of hot water and a splash of oil.

In a small clean pan melt a little more butter and, quickly but carefully, lightly brown the scallops. Add them to the pan of fennel. Add the sauce to the pan of scallops and fennel. Make sure everything is hot.

Finish by cooking the chopped corals in the residue of butter in the scallop pan.

Check for seasoning and give a squeeze of lemon if required. Place a little of the pasta on 4 hot plates, top with the fennel, scallops and sauce. Finish by scattering over the coral and chopped fresh fennel leaves.

Serve immediately – not forgetting the champagne!

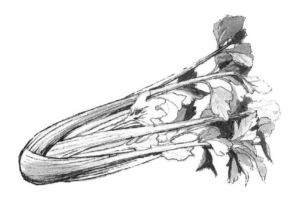

Rabbit Legs stuffed with Boudin Noir and Prunes

For four

1 tablespoon olive oil, plus extra for drizzling

1 shallot, finely chopped

2 tender stalks of celery, finely chopped

30g pancetta or smoked bacon, finely chopped

113g of French boudin noir, skin removed

60g soft mi-cuit prunes, well chopped

1 tablespoon fresh white breadcrumbs

1 tablespoon pine nuts

½ teaspoon (or to taste) French quatre-épices

freshly ground black pepper

cognac

Maldon sea salt

4 plump rabbit legs (French farmed ideally), thigh bone removed

8 thin rashers of smoked bacon, rinds removed

1 wine glass of Noilly Prat* or other dry white wine)

1 teaspoon of concentrated chicken stock** or half a chicken stock cube

water

30g butter, cold

Preheat the oven to 200C/Gas 6.

In a pan heat the olive oil gently. Add the shallot and celery and cook over a medium heat for 2 minutes. Add the bacon bits, stir round and cook for another couple of minutes. Add the boudin noir, prunes, breadcrumbs, pine nuts, quatre-épices and plenty of black pepper. Mix everything well. Add a splash of cognac and a little more olive oil if you think it needs it. Taste and season. Put the stuffing in the fridge to harden up a bit while you prepare the rabbit.

The rabbit leg will contain the thigh bone and the leg bone. Gently break the joint between the two and then with the help a small, sharp, pointed knife separate the thigh bone from the surrounding flesh and ease it out, trying not to break the skin. Ultimately you will end up with four legs each with a pocket. Fill each pocket with the stuffing. Make the legs plump but don't overfill. Now stretch each rasher of bacon using the flat of a knife and wrap two rashers round each leg making sure that the bacon covers the pocket opening.

Place the legs in a roasting pan, drizzle with olive oil and bake for around 20-25 minutes. Remove to a warm dish and allow to rest in the turned off oven while you make the gravy and plate up.

Pour off any excess oil left in the roasting pan. Pour in the wine glass of Noilly Prat, stir it round and over a medium heat reduce by about half. Add concentrated chicken stock and a little water. Taste. Cook for a few minutes. Bring to the boil and stir in the cold chopped butter, a few pieces at a time, to give the sauce a sheen and rich flavour. Check the seasoning.

Place a leg on each of 4 heated plates. Slice the thigh into 4 even slices so the stuffing is exposed. Drizzle a little of the gravy over the meat and pour the rest into a jug to put on the table.

I would serve some buttery potato and celeriac mash and small lightly cooked French beans to accompany.

(*See My Store Cupboard Favourites, p.238, ** p.234)

Fillet of Roe Deer with Foie Gras

This is one of my 'ultimate' dishes – you know when you think, at the end of a meal, things can't really get much better this. It's dead easy to cook yet ideal for a special occasion. If you had it in a restaurant it would cost an arm and a leg. Cooked at home? Not quite so much! This recipe is one of the reasons why I like to buy uncooked foie gras from Nelly Vatel.

If you do manage to get hold of a whole lobe of uncooked foie gras then here is what I suggest you do: remove it from its packaging, then with a very sharp knife dipped into hot water cut the lobe crossways into slices about 4cm thick. Remove any fibrous bits with your sharp knife, wrap each slice firmly in cling film and replace in the fridge until ready to use.

Farmed roe deer is inexpensive, incredibly tender and very tasty without being too 'gamey'. You definitely need to like pinkish meat. If you are into seriously well-cooked steak then there's not much point in cooking this.

I would serve the roe deer fillet topped with the foie gras on a bed of crisp spring cabbage mixed with buttered leeks served with a rich fruity gravy. And, if it is a really special meal, individual casseroles of dauphinois potatoes. Otherwise just some really good bread to mop it all up with.

The final minute or two of finishing everything and getting it all hot onto the plates can be a bit frantic; it pays to be very well organised. I find it best not to drink too much wine when I am preparing this dish!

For two
  2 x 4cm thick slices of raw foie gras
  2 x 170g fillets of roe deer
  Maldon salt and freshly ground black pepper
  olive oil
  1 shallot, finely chopped
  small glass red wine (Côtes du Rhône is good)

140ml good game or beef stock

2-3 juniper berries, crushed

a dash of Madeira

redcurrant jelly to taste

½ small pointed cabbage, centre removed, thinly sliced

90g butter

2-3 young leeks, white part only, chopped into 3cm lengths

squeeze of lemon

About 10 minutes before you intend to cook them remove two slices of foie gras from the fridge.

Allow the roe deer fillets to come up to room temperature. Season with salt and pepper and massage all over with a little olive oil.

Make sure you remember to heat the plates.

Preheat oven 180C/Gas 4.

Make the gravy first – at least up to the point of adding in the butter. Put the chopped shallot into a small saucepan, add the wine and bring to the boil. Reduce the wine by about half. Add the stock and the crushed juniper berries. Cook for around 20 minutes allowing the liquid to reduce by around a quarter. Taste and add a dash of the Madeira and a teaspoon of redcurrant jelly. Cook together for a few minutes and check for strength and flavour. Add more wine, Madeira or redcurrant jelly to get a good balance. Strain and leave the sauce to one side to complete later.

Put the cabbage in a saucepan with some salt. Pour over enough boiling water to cover, bring to the boil and cook for no more than two minutes. Drain and quickly cool in cold water. Drain again. Leave to one side.

Melt 30g butter in a shallow sided pan. Add the leeks and fry gently until soft. Increase the heat slightly to lightly colour then add the cabbage. Stir together, season well and cook for a further minute or two. Tip into an ovenproof dish, cover with foil and put on a bottom shelf in the warm oven.

Have a really hot griddle pan ready on the top of the stove and a hot dish in the oven. Sear the roe deer fillets on a high heat – about 2 minutes on each side. Transfer them to the dish in the oven where they will cook for further 10 minutes. Remove from the oven, cover with foil and a folded tea towel and leave to rest.

Bring the sauce to the boil and pour in any residues from the resting fillets. Add in the cold chopped butter, a few bits at a time, whisking well until the sauce thickens slightly and has a sheen. Taste – season again if necessary adding a squeeze of lemon if it seems a little sweet.

Have the hot plates ready. Make a bed of cabbage and leek on each and place the fillet on top. Turn off the oven and open the door. Slip the two plates into the oven while you finish the foie gras.

Making sure the griddle is red hot, place the seasoned slices of foie gras on it and cook for no more than 30 seconds per side. The liver should bear the marks of the griddle, have some slightly caramelised bits and be just beginning to melt. Place it immediately on top of the roe deer fillet. Pour a little gravy over. Serve the rest in a jug.

Garnish with some chopped chives and a sprig of redcurrants if you have them.

Serve immediately.

Celebration Champagne Risotto

This is essentially the classic Italian Risotto alla Milanese given a festive touch. Not only does it taste delicious but the dramatic presentation causes a bit of glitzy excitement. I like it with plenty of lightly cooked fresh tips of asparagus folded in at the last minute and (obviously) served with an accompanying glass or two of champagne.

For four

> *1½ litre well-flavoured vegetable stock (ideally home-made but Marigold is fine. I also make up the stock using the asparagus water. If you wish to do this then do not add salt to the asparagus cooking water)*
>
> *1kg fresh green or white asparagus*
>
> *100g unsalted butter*
>
> *2 tablespoons good-quality virgin olive oil*
>
> *4 large shallots peeled and finely chopped*
>
> *110ml dry champagne*
>
> *350g Vialone Nano risotto rice*
>
> *Maldon sea salt and and freshly ground black pepper*
>
> *60-80g butter*
>
> *100g aged Parmesan finely grated*

To serve

> *20cl bottle champagne (at room temperature)*
>
> *½ sugar lump*

Bring the stock to a boil in a saucepan, reduce the heat to keep it just below simmering point.

Peel the asparagus stems with a potato peeler and then break each stem at its natural breaking point. Put in a large pan and pour on boiling water. Throw in some salt. Cook for a few minutes making sure that the asparagus is just al dente. Drain and cool quickly. Cut the tips from the stalks and put to one side to add to the risotto later. Keep the stems for another dish.

Meanwhile, melt the butter and oil together in a wide, shallow heavy-bottomed pan. (I must admit to a bias towards my cast-iron Le Creuset pots, which are the ideal for making risotto.) Add the chopped shallots and sauté for 5 minutes until soft but not brown. Add 6 tablespoons of the stock to the shallots, along with the champagne. Heat until the mixture is reduced by half. Add the rice and cook on a medium heat stirring continuously until the wine and stock are absorbed. Continue to add the stock a ladleful at a time, stirring the rice between each addition. The rice needs to absorb most of the liquid before you add the next ladleful. This process takes patience – you must constantly stir the rice. The rice will take about 20 to 30 minutes to cook. The grains should be tender though still with a little bite at their centre

Remove from the heat, fold in the butter and the Parmesan and beat well. Add the asparagus tips and mix in gently. Check the seasoning. This final part needs to be done fairly quickly as you want the risotto to be very hot. Transfer the risotto to a preheated deep-sided bowl. Scatter over a few more asparagus tips and finish with more Parmesan. Make a small well in the centre of the risotto. Wipe the bottle of champagne with a dry cloth, uncork, drop the sugar lump into the neck, and quickly place it in the 'well'. Bring the dish to the table. The bubbles will spray out and then drip down onto the risotto. Once your guests' 'oohs' and 'aahs' have died down, remove the bottle and any remains, turn the risotto once or twice so that it absorbs the champagne. Serve the risotto to your guests with an accompanying glass of fizz.

Alternatively instead of the asparagus (or even, if you are really pushing the boat out, as well as) cook some peeled langoustines (5 or 6 for each person) quickly in some butter with a small clove of crushed garlic and some parsley. Keep the langoustines warm (remove the crushed garlic). Once the champagne bottle has been removed, spoon over the langoustines and the buttery juices. Finish with a scattering of parsley or finely chopped chives.

Champagne and Elderflower Jelly

Elder trees and bushes are endemic to the towpath. The elderflowers appear in late spring. The individual flowers are so small, so sweet and delicate; I just love to make a trail of them across the top of a jelly just before it has set. If you are making this outside of the elderflower season then an alternative bit of glamour would be to stir, very carefully, a shimmer of edible gold leaf powder into the jelly just before the setting is complete so that it is suspended throughout the body of the jelly.

For six

> *5 sheets gelatine*
> *100ml water*
> *75cl champagne or sparkling wine*
> *75g caster sugar*
> *2 tablespoons elderflower cordial*

Soak the gelatine in cold water until softened. Pour 100ml of water and about a quarter of the champagne into a saucepan and add the caster sugar. Heat gently until the sugar has dissolved. Squeeze the excess water from the gelatine sheets and stir them into the syrup until they have melted away. Strain into a bowl and leave until cool. Add the rest of the champagne and the cordial stirring well. Divide the jelly between 6 champagne glasses. Chill for about 4 hours (or overnight) to set.

Serve with a jug of pouring cream on the side.

CHAPTER 9

Barging into Burgundy

Hello, is anyone still reading this? I do hope so, although it is possible that some will probably have switched off after the third or fourth reference to champagne guzzling, not forgetting either, the wittering on about foie gras. And I see I've even managed to throw in a mention of scallops and roe deer fillets.

'Blimey – who does she think she is?' I hear you say. 'Lady Muck?'

'Everyone knows she's bog-Irish'

'More Mrs O'Bucket then than Mrs O'Bouquet.'

Hard perhaps to believe, but we really are very humble boaters and not much given to unseemly displays of over-indulgence – well, not often.

In fact having now seen the latest credit card statement there will be no more indulging of any kind for quite some time. It's bread and scrape from now on.

Luckily for us and our bank balance, since the outing to Champagne we have been on the move and mostly living off free food courtesy of lock-keepers and whatever I have been able to forage along the towpath and in nearby fields. Luckily too, this is the time of year when the French bombard us with the abundance of their gardens. A lettuce, a cucumber, some radishes, tomatoes, green beans and even eggs have been left, at various times, on the deck by the wheelhouse door. Rarely does anyone knock to say 'here you are – this is for you'.

News comes to say that our preferred route south to Burgundy from Condé is to be closed soon due to lack of water. We decide to take the 'Heuilley' canal instead. This is the boatman's name for the Canal Marne à la Saône, now renamed in the interests of tourism: the Champagne to Burgundy Canal. It is a more direct way, only 70 engine hours and 130 locks (whew) but we need to allow for at least a couple of weeks, or more, on the move. This waterway is so far off the beaten track that we are unlikely to find anywhere to buy food once we are underway. Before leaving it is necessary to do a big boring shop at the Carrefour in Chalons-en-Champagne but I make up for that by insisting on a final visit to the 'pick-your-own-farm' at Aulney-sur-Marne.

We collect our wheelbarrow and secateurs from the shed next to the shop and start following the signs. 'Tomatoes,' I say, 'Look, it says they have ancient breeds down there. We won't pick too many, though it's nice to have them so fresh.' First we divert along the courgette rows and burrowing under the leaves find lots of them, yellow and green, young and firm. Then on to the tomatoes which are grown outside. I pick loads of the variety called Andine Cornue; they are wonderful: huge, fleshy, deeply red and irresistible; in no time at all we have snipped off several kilos. I've never seen the little vine tomatoes actually growing before so when I spot a whole hedge of them – and then taste them – I feel impelled to add yet another kilo or so to our load. The wheelbarrow now has some weight to it and Captain begins to mutter things like 'it's only us don't forget'. We trundle off towards the rows of fresh herbs: tarragon, chives, parsley, basil and thyme; I gather an assorted job lot but only get charged for one bunch: about 50 euro-cents.

Then I see a small notice announcing that the Deberastavel apples are ready for picking. This is my favourite apple when eaten straight from the tree: crisp, sweet and juicy and surely the very one with which Eve must have tempted Adam. Sadly, once picked, they lose their wonderful fresh effervescence after a few days in the fruit bowl, but that brief moment of perfection when the apple is hanging there, ripe and ready, is something to look forward to each year. I walk along munching happily and feel obliged to put several more into the barrow.

Next day, early, we finally wave goodbye to Condé, turn left at the junction and head along the, initially, not terribly exciting Canal Latéral à la Marne. We will stay more or less next to the Marne all the way to its source which bubbles up close to the tunnel on the summit level near Langres in the Haute Marne. Later as the waterway becomes smaller and increasingly rural it gets more wind-y, passing close to a succession of villages filled with simple rustic buildings so beautiful that they make you want to weep. Everywhere you look there is something delightful to behold. What one sees can never be replicated in a photograph: sunlight dappling through an old vine; sparkling water in a mill stream; endless avenues of ancient trees lining the canal; far better to forget capturing them on camera and try, instead, to fix such images in the mind's eye, there to be treasured forever.

As always when we set out I have enough food on board to feed a small army should one happen by or to withstand a siege were that on the cards. Who knows – be prepared I say! We decide not to stop at all at Vitry-le-Francois which is the last big town where we can stock up with provisions. The lock just before the town tells its own story, surrounded as it is by a high wire fence with coils of barbed wire strategically placed. We view the gang of youths standing on the foot-bridge above the lock with some trepidation. I point the camera at them and say *'bonjour'*. With some relief we leave the lock and Vitry behind us, turn right at the junction, and press on towards a safer haven on the Marne à la Saône canal beyond.

As we go, I slow-roast some of the tomatoes with garlic and thyme to make the base for a pasta sauce and yet more ratatouille; it will keep in the fridge for several days and provide fairly instant meals on the days when my Captain forgets we are supposed to be on holiday and we tie up late. I hollow out the centres of a couple of big, ripe tomatoes and stuff them with leftover rice, chopped ham and fresh herbs for tonight's dinner. All the seeds, pulp and juice that I have removed, I leave to drain in a muslin-lined sieve thinking I might make an elegant cold tomato consommé, though the next day I use it all up in a fabulous tomato risotto which we have with freshwater crayfish bought from a man with a bucket and a bicycle who I meet on the towpath.

I am glad that I did make the basis for several meals as we travelled along that first stretch of not-so-exciting waterway because from now on it gets increasingly more attractive and interesting and the weather is improving no end; cooking (believe it or not) becomes less appealing. We stop more often, relax in the sun, swim in the canal, walk and explore, and generally begin to feel in a bit of a holiday mood.

As usual, once we have moored up, I grab a bag and mosey off along the towpath to see what I can find. Right now, in late August, we are betwixt and between. The wild asparagus is over, the elderflowers are turning into berries, the tiny strawberries that hide in the undergrowth have all but disappeared and the birds have long finished off the cherries. It's too early yet for the hard fruits, the nuts, the berries and mushrooms but I keep a weather eye on their development and mostly know where the best are to be found.

For now I must content myself with wild oregano and apple scented mint, borage, sweet cicely and wild fennel fronds. I make a bouquet and stick them in a jam jar. I'll add them fresh to salads and to jugs of Pimms or use them to make refreshing tisanes.

We tie up often and wander through any number of small villages en route and note the paucity of bakers, grocery shops and restaurants. Places that our ancient *'Carte Fluviale'* shows as supplying such services but that do so no longer. With the result that when we do find a small shop, a bar serving as a *depot de pain* or an actual restaurant we are very keen to show our support and buy something.

It is salutary to see how many canal-side villages exist today without commerce of any kind. Once there would have been a 'Café de la Marine' at almost every lock (which went some way to explaining the permanent air of tipsiness found among many lock-keepers at the time), as well as a general provisions shop supplying all the needs of the barging community. There would have been lock-keepers – dozens of them. Local people would have been permanently employed to look after the horses which towed the boats; there were farriers, suppliers of fodder and stabling; providers too of both the horse and manpower required to move the barges along the canal. Boatyards, barge builders and workshops would be located at every canal junction. Wharves, where once dozens of men were employed loading and unloading barges armed with little more than brute strength, shovels and wheelbarrows, are still just discernible in the undergrowth or have taken on a new lease of life as stopping places for pleasure craft. But they are empty of people; no longer swarming with life. Sadly even the numerous silos that sit beside so many waterways do not use barges to transport their contents any longer.

We looked at the huge barns that once housed the hundreds of tons of grain, maize and other products harvested from the land every year by those who dwelt here and wondered at the changes wrought upon rural life over the years. The buildings still stand but the trade and the people have long gone.

Our barging is a slow sort of activity with many hours spent meandering along virtually deserted canals and rivers. We do have time to stand and stare and wonder at the passing of life; hours are spent in conjecture: why was that warehouse there; what activities took place here; how must the canal once have been and where have all the barges gone? Conjecture kicks in once again as we try to envisage that busy canal world of yesteryear from the perspective of today.

The towpaths once populated by horses pulling barges now have a new role as long-distance cycle tracks for holidaymakers and aspirational entrants to the Tour de France. Holidaymakers are fine, but the lycra-clad brigade streaming along beside us, eyes firmly focussed at handlebar level, are a complete anathema to me. Having given up on ever taking the perfect 'heron in flight' pic I decide to turn my photographing attention to the towpath users instead; I find I have as great a problem snapping the speeding cyclist as I have the flying heron.

So do the long days pass.

We approach lock Saint-Maurice on the Heuilley Canal. Captain zaps it with his telecommand and it begins to fill for us. As we get closer we register several things more or less simultaneously: there's a perfect place to moor on the offside above the lock; café chairs and tables laid for a meal are arranged under an awning directly outside the lock cottage; a notice and arrow point to a goat farm just across the road.

It's an air punching moment –YES….stop, stop, stop!

Friesland is put into rapid reverse and we back away from the lock. Problem is though, the lock has been activated and is now getting ready for us. If we don't go through it and thus complete the locking cycle it will automatically switch itself off after about 20 minutes, then no one else can use it until the traveling VNF man in his little white van is alerted and turns up to re-activate it. Were we to go through we know there will be nowhere sensible to tie below the lock so the rare opportunity this canal affords by way of a good mooring, a restaurant meal, and an artisan maker of cheese, all at one and the same time, will be missed.

What to do? We decide to stop and make instead a 'virtual' passage through the lock. The lock has filled and the gates are open awaiting *Friesland's* arrival. We quickly tie up, and armed with a large cork mat, leap off the boat and head towards the lock. Captain passes the mat slowly in front of the electronic beam positioned just before the open gates. This is to simulate the entry of a boat into the lock so that the next stage of the lock working is activated. Then, using the telecommand, he zaps the lock again and the gates shut behind our phantom barge; the lock empties and the bottom gates slowly swing open. Now he goes down the steps to just beyond the gates and passes the mat, once again, across a second beam, which then registers a boat leaving the lock. Our ghost boat exits the lock and the cycle is completed when the bottom gates shut behind it. All is well: the lock is now ready and waiting for any other boats to come along; we can return to our nice mooring above the lock and the clever cork mat will be tucked back into its drawer.

Next we call in at the lock house and book ourselves a table *'au terrasse'* for that evening, before heading across the road to the farm. Here we discover they are having an open day; you can feed the goats, help with the milking and see how the cheese is made. Small children mill around clutching pans of goat food which they throw nervously into the faces of the very inquisitive kids. An aggressive ram is intent upon butting anyone who comes too close and an ancient fellow, looking for all the world like a bewhiskered Chinaman, wanders free and patiently allows himself to be stroked by all the children.

The downside of all of this excitement is that the small farm shop has very little cheese left to sell. I buy enough of the *moyen* – not too young and soft, not too old and dry – to make a salad of *chèvre chaud* for lunch the following day.

On our way back to *Friesland* we see an empty barge coming into the lock. We wait until it has risen up to the top and then go over to talk to its very young Dutch skipper who we can see was obviously not born to the life. We tell him of the barge, the *Vite*, which we had met at Condé, also Dutch, with another very young owner. 'Yes, yes,' he says, 'he is a friend and only nineteen years old – three years younger than me.' Just as we were, in our own youth, they are entranced by the barging life and prepared to work very hard to keep the canal alive with freight for a bit longer. We ask him how ones so young can afford to buy such beautiful ships? He is airily nonchalant in his reply – 'The bank lends us the money – it's no problem.' He has just discharged 250 tonnes of Canadian mustard seed at Dijon and says he is now on his way back to Reims where he is hoping to load steel coils for Antwerp.

Back to the boat with our spoils from the farm, then it's time for a spruce-up before we amble the twenty yards or so across the grass to our dinner. We are seated outside, beside the lock, under the awning. It's a balmy evening and although this is the middle of the week the rest of the tables soon fill up with what I can only imagine are all local people as everyone seems to know everyone else. We are each brought a Kir – the apéritif is on the house and made with their own blackberry liqueur; it's a kind gesture and gets us off to a good start. The menu is limited and surprise, surprise, features a fair amount of goats' cheese in various forms, including, as a starter, the aforementioned *Salade de chèvre chaud*. Captain chooses instead the home-made terrine and I order six *escargots*. This is followed by *tartiflette* with a green salad fresh from the garden beside the lock. Dessert is a delicious, and again home-made, crème caramel. We drink a bottle of simple Burgundy red and finish with a cafetière of coffee. A good meal with friendly service in a pleasant setting for a very few euros – what's not to enjoy?

It is dark when we leave our table at the end of the meal; a lamp set high up on the side of the lock house is thoughtfully switched on and sees us safely back to the boat.

RECIPES

There are some things you just can't live without – imagine a world without tomatoes. Because I love them so much I try not to buy them once their natural season is over; when you have tasted ones grown outside in the fresh air, fleshed out by rain and ripened naturally in the sunshine – then, like apricots and asparagus, you are willing to wait until it is time. For the rest of the year I am happy to use good tinned or better still, my own preserved passata.

Summer Tomato Consommé

This is a classic dish and the perfect summer starter for when a) you have loads of ripe tomatoes, b) guests to impress, c) enough time on your hands to warrant a bit of fiddling about. This cold clear soup does take a little time although it is not at all complicated; on the other hand it can be made well in advance, left in the fridge until needed or even frozen for another time.

For four
> *4 tablespoons olive oil*
> *2 large spring onions finely chopped*
> *1kg large ripe juicy tomatoes roughly chopped*
> *2 cloves garlic crushed and creamed with a little Maldon sea salt*
> *1 teaspoon each of basil. chervil and tarragon, finely chopped*
> *1 teaspoon Maldon sea salt*
> *1 - 1½ teaspoons caster sugar*
> *4 egg whites*
> *¼ teaspoon each of black and white peppercorns.*

In a wide shallow-sided pan gently heat the olive oil. Add the onions and sweat for a minute or two. Add three-quarters of the tomatoes plus the garlic, herbs, salt and sugar. Cook over a medium heat for 10-15 minutes until it looks pulpy, stirring frequently. Pour in a litre of water and bring to the boil. Simmer for around 20 minutes, skimming off any froth that forms.

Line a colander or large sieve with a square of wet muslin (or a thin clean tea towel). Set it over a deep bowl and pour the liquid tomato through, pressing down any debris with the back of a spoon in order to collect as much of the intensely flavoured juice as possible.

Cool quickly by standing the bowl of tomato liquid in a basin filled with cold water and ice.

Whizz the remaining chopped tomatoes with the egg whites and peppercorns in a food processor. Tip this messy looking stuff into a large saucepan and add the cooled tomato juice. Bring the saucepan slowly to the boil and simmer for around 20 minutes. Once the liquid is crystal clear pour it again into the colander lined with another square of clean wet muslin (or tea towel). This time do not press with the spoon. Just let it drip through. If it is a little cloudy pass it through the rinsed muslin again.

Chill until ready to serve or freeze for another time.

Lightly cook a few green vegetables – mange tout, tiny French beans, baby broad beans and asparagus tips. Allow to cool, then slice them into short pieces, scatter in the bottom of four bowls and pour over the clear consommé. I sometimes add ready-cooked crayfish (langoustines). Remove from their shells and place two or three in each bowl as well. Finish with a little drizzle of olive oil on the surface and a scattering of chervil leaves.

Tomato Tarts

These are delicious and if you use shop-bought puff pastry, very quick to make. Good as a starter with a few leaves of rocket or purslane and a teaspoonful of pesto or for lunch with a more substantial green salad on the side.

For four

> *2 tablespoons fresh white breadcrumbs*
> *2 tablespoons Parmesan, finely grated*
> *30g soft butter*
> *1 packet of all-butter puff pastry*
> *2 or 3 medium-sized ripe tomatoes*
> *salt, pepper and a pinch of sugar.*

You will also need four non-stick individual tart tins with removable bases

In a bowl mix the breadcrumbs and Parmesan together.

Lightly grease the interiors of the tart tins with some of the soft butter.

Using something slightly bigger than the tins as a template cut out four circles of pastry. Line each tin with a circle, press the pastry down gently and don't worry if the sides are a bit untidy. Once cooked it gives the pastry a slightly rustic look which suits these tarts.

Prick the bases lightly and place all four in the fridge for about 10 minutes

Preheat the oven to 200C/Gas 6

Thinly slice the tomatoes onto a plate

Remove tart shells from fridge and quickly spread a good layer of breadcrumbs and cheese over each base. Now carefully place the tomatoes on top, making a neat circle and over-lapping them as you go. Finish with a round in the middle. Melt the rest of the butter and with a pastry brush lightly paint over the tomatoes and any exposed pastry. Season well and scatter a pinch of sugar over each tart.

Place them in the centre of the oven and bake for about 15 minutes until the pastry is crisp and golden. Remove from oven and leave to cool for a few minutes.

Transfer the tarts from the tins to individual plates. Serve warm.

A Perfect Tomato Salad

The secret of a good tomato salad is to remember that the dressing needs to be quite intense as it will become diluted by all the tomato juices in the salad. Once it has mixed with the tomatoes it should be perfectly balanced so that you will want to use your bread to mop up any left-over dressing in the salad bowl.

Ideally use locally sourced, outdoor grown tomatoes of all shapes and colours. Failing the ideal, go for the ripest, tastiest, juiciest tomatoes you can find. There's no place here for out-of-season hydroponically grown ones.

For this sort of salad I like my tomatoes to be chunkily sliced or if small cut into quarters.

For four
> *1 kg tomatoes*
> *1 medium red onion, thinly sliced*
> *a handful of fresh basil leaves, torn into bits*
> *salt and pepper*
> *sugar*

For the dressing
> *1 fat clove garlic*
> *Maldon sea salt*

1 teaspoon Dijon mustard
1 tablespoon light runny honey (acacia is good)
1 tablespoon white wine vinegar
cold-pressed extra virgin olive oil

Cut up the tomatoes into juicy chunks and put them into a salad bowl. Add the onion and the basil. Season with salt, pepper and a pinch of sugar. Gently mix everything together.

Make the dressing: crush the garlic with the flat of a knife. Put it into a mortar with a good pinch of Maldon sea salt and using the pestle cream the two together. Add the mustard, honey and vinegar and again use the pestle to mix everything together. Now add the olive oil, just a little at a time, mixing it well. Taste to make sure there is both sweetness, saltiness and acidity. It needs to be quite full-on as the tomato juice in the salad will dilute it. Too much olive oil will make the dressing bland. Give it a good stir and the dressing will emulsify and look quite thick. Pour it into a small, lidded jar – you may not need to use it all – and give it a good shake.

Spoon a generous amount of the dressing over the tomatoes just before the salad is served and mix well.

When we have tomato salad for lunch I usually serve it, with a mild goats' cheese, Greek feta or burrata and lots of good bread to mop up the juices.

Roast Tomato Risotto with Crayfish

This tastes wonderful made with really ripe tomatoes. My preference is to use half-and-half of ripe round tomatoes that contain plenty of juice and the much fleshier plum type like the glorious Andine Cornue. Whatever you use though – even good Italian tinned is fine – has to be of the finest quality; watery under-ripe tomatoes just will not do.

You can buy cooked shelled crayfish tails in most good fishmongers or supermarkets these days. I used a 250g packet of them for this recipe.

This makes about 500ml of sauce. Leftovers can be used as a base for a pasta sauce. It will keep happily in the fridge for a few days or frozen until you need it.

For two to four

> *½-¾ litre of chicken stock (Knorr Concentrated is fine* - see p.234)*
>
> *250ml roast tomato sauce*
>
> *25g unsalted butter*
>
> *1 tablespoon olive oil*
>
> *1 small shallot, peeled and very finely chopped*
>
> *Maldon sea salt and freshly ground black pepper*
>
> *bay leaves*
>
> *175g arborio rice*
>
> *25g Parmesan, freshly finely grated, plus more for the table*
>
> *1 clove garlic, crushed*
>
> *a little parsley, chopped*
>
> *250g of cooked peeled crayfish tails*

Roast Tomato Sauce

> *75g chopped onion*
>
> *3-4 tablespoons olive oil*
>
> *1 kg ripe tomatoes, halved lengthways*
>
> *Maldon sea salt and freshly ground black pepper*
>
> *several fresh sprigs of lemon thyme*

1-2 teaspoons caster sugar

4 cloves garlic, unpeeled but crushed with the flat of a heavy knife

1 bay leaf

Preheat the oven to 180C/Gas 4

Make the roast tomato sauce first: place the chopped onions in a small bowl and add just a dribble of the olive oil. Mix it into the onions with your hand so they are well-coated. Leave to one side

Lay the halved tomatoes cut-side up on a lightly oiled baking tray. Sprinkle them liberally with salt, pepper, olive oil, thyme and the sugar. Tuck the garlic cloves and the bay leaf in around them. Bake for an hour then scatter the onion over the tomatoes.

Cook for a further 30 minutes until the tomatoes are soft and collapsed. When cool enough to handle, remove the garlic skins and discard the bay leaf. Liquidise everything together then pass through a sieve. Check the seasoning.

To make the risotto: in a large saucepan, combine the stock and tomato sauce and bring to a gentle simmer. Keep it simmering on the back of the stove while you prepare the risotto.

In a large heavy bottomed pan melt the butter, add the olive oil, the shallot, a good pinch of salt and the bay leaves. Cook over a moderate heat stirring the shallot until it is soft and translucent. Add the rice and stir until it is well coated with the oils and becoming glistening and slightly translucent - about 2 or 3 minutes. Add a ladleful of the simmering stock. Stir constantly until the rice has nearly absorbed all the stock before adding more. Continue to add the stock a ladleful at a time, stirring all the while. Do this until the rice is almost tender but still has a little bite to it. This can take anything from 20 to 30 minutes. The finished rice should have a creamy porridge-like consistency.

Remove the pan from the heat and stir in the butter and cheese. Cover and leave for a couple of minutes.

Melt a little butter in a pan, add a crushed finely chopped clove of garlic and a good tablespoon of chopped parsley. Cook gently for a minute or two and then add the crayfish tails. Stir them around long enough to be warmed and well-coated with the garlic butter.

Serve the risotto in warm bowls and top each serving with the crayfish.

Put an additional bowl of grated Parmesan on the table.

Bruschetta with Red Onions and Goats' Cheese

Bruschetta, as you probably know, is the Italian name for thick slices of grilled or oven-dried bread that is rubbed with garlic, drizzled with olive oil and then topped with all manner of tasty bits and pieces. This recipe is a nicely rustic starter to a simple Italian meal or a tasty lunch with a green side salad.

For one

> *4 tablespoons olive oil*
> *25g butter*
> *2 medium red onions, thickly sliced*
> *1 tablespoon balsamic vinegar*
> *4 black olives, stoned and chopped*
> *a few fresh thyme leaves*
> *2 tinned anchovy fillets, chopped*

50g goats' cheese
1 or 2 thick slices of a ciabatta loaf
1 clove of garlic

Heat 1 tablespoon of olive oil and the butter in a small frying pan. Gently sauté the onions to soften. After about 5 minutes raise the heat and once the onions start to wilt and colour add the balsamic vinegar. Continue to cook until the vinegar has nearly all evaporated. Stir in the olives, thyme leaves and anchovies and cook for a few minutes while you organise the bruschetta. Toast the bread on one side until just lightly golden and then rub that side with garlic. Turn it over and sprinkle well with the remaining olive oil. Grill until the oiled side is nicely brown then turn once again and finish the other side.

Cover with the onion mixture and a couple of rounds of goats' cheese on top. Flash under the hot grill until the cheese begins to bubble and melt.

Lift onto a warm plate and eat immediately.

Simple Goats' Cheese Soufflé

I found the recipe for this soufflé in *Sally Clarke's Book* years ago and it is one that I have made often. Those who swear they hate goats' cheese will eat this very happily as the only cheesy taste is that of Parmesan. This soufflé doesn't rise as high as the traditional one nor flop so far either. I usually only make it for two; any more than that and they have to be spread over two shelves in the oven and they don't cook uniformly enough to serve all together. As soon as you start opening and closing oven doors soufflés get sulky and won't perform, so save this dish just for yourself and your dearest friend. I like to eat it with nothing more than a bit of fresh baguette to mop up the cheesy juices.

The soufflé is best cooked in a small round shallow-sided dish – I use the ovenproof ones which have two little ears to hold them by.

For two

>*10g unsalted butter, melted*
>*140g Parmesan, freshly grated*
>*2 fresh free range eggs, separated*
>*135g fresh soft goats' cheese*
>*50ml double cream*
>*½ teaspoon chopped thyme*
>*sea salt and freshly ground black pepper*

Preheat the oven to 200C/Gas 6

Butter two ovenproof soup plates or cocottes and sprinkle with a little of the grated Parmesan, just to coat the insides.

Whisk the egg yolks until smooth, add the goats' cheese and whisk again. Stir in the cream and season with some of the chopped thyme, salt and pepper. Fold in half of the remaining Parmesan. In a separate, clean dry bowl whisk the whites with a pinch of salt until stiff peaks are formed. Fold the whites carefully but thoroughly into the cheese mixture, divide between the dishes and sprinkle with the rest of the thyme leaves and remaining Parmesan. Place on a baking sheet in the oven and bake until risen and golden (approximately 8 to 10 minutes).

Serve immediately, remembering to warn your fellow diner that the dishes are oven hot.

Blackberry Liqueur

I always have a bottle of this in the cupboard; not only to make a refreshing Kir but a dash added to a berry-based fruit salad or to a bowl of cooked pears always gives a special extra flavour boost.

1kg blackberries
1 litre good red wine (I like a fruity Beaujolais)
about 1½kg white sugar
¾ litre vodka

Steep the blackberries in the wine for 48 hours. Line a large basin (or washing up bowl) with a piece of old clean sheeting. Gradually feed the fruit and wine into a liquidiser or processor and then tip into the cloth-lined basin. Draw the cloth together and twist it tightly to squeeze all the liquid from the mush into the basin.

Measure the liquid and for every litre add 1kg of sugar. Note the level. Pour into a pan, place over a low heat and stir until all the sugar has dissolved. Use a thermometer to check the heat – it needs to be above blood temperature (36.5C) but well below simmering or boiling. Set a timer for 15 minutes. Then check the temperature of the liquid and give it a thorough stir. Do this several times more, slowly increasing the intervals. In about 2 hours the level should have dropped a little and the liquid become slightly syrupy. Leave to cool.

Into a clean bowl, pour one mug of vodka and add three mugs of blackberry syrup. Repeat until all the syrup is used, adjusting the quantities appropriately towards the end in the ratio of 1:3. Using a funnel, pour into sterilised bottles and seal. Leave for at least a week or two before broaching.

This recipe can be used in exactly the same way to make a blackcurrant liqueur. It comes from *Jane Grigson's Fruit Book* and she recommends a mix of Perrier water, cassis and ice for a refreshingly long and rather less alcoholic drink than the traditional Kir.

Pears in Red Wine

Small hard pears work best in this simple recipe. On some canals where the lock houses have been abandoned you will often come across these old pear trees in what's left of the garden. Hop off the boat and grab a few. If there are plenty then take a few more than you think you need as they do bottle very well.

Peel them thinly, leave the stalks on and cut a thin slice from the base of the pear so that it will stand up. Place them shoulder to shoulder in a fireproof dish. Make a syrup of two parts light brown sugar to one of water. Add one star anise or a small cinnamon stick. Pour equal quantities of the syrup and red wine into the dish so that it just tops the pears. Cover with a lid and cook in a really low oven (150C/Gas 2) for at least a couple of hours until the pears are soft, almost translucent and have coloured to a beautiful crimson.

Reduce any liquid to a syrupy consistency by boiling it in a small pan. Cool and taste – if too sweet, add a drop of lemon juice. Serve the pears and syrup very cold with a bowl of crème fraîche to hand.

Griottines in Armagnac

These are a very sharp bright red cherry. Too sharp for a dessert cherry; even the birds leave them alone. If you've never tried your hand at bottling before, try this; the reward for such a simple task is huge – just how I like it.

Sterilise some Kilner jars. Just boil them up in some water. Fish them out and let them dry. Immediately fill with the cherries, which you have washed, pricking each one 3 or 4 times with a cocktail stick and trimming the stalks, leaving about 12mm on each cherry.

Almost fill the jars with the cherries. Pour in enough caster sugar to come up about a third of the jar and then enough armagnac to cover the fruit.

Seal and leave in a cool dark place for as many years as you can stand to wait – but one year is the bare minimum. Help dissolve the sugar by turning the jars upside down from time to time.

CHAPTER 10

Time for a Truffle or Two

Canals are not the most obvious place to go looking for fungi but Christmas came early for us this year as we were boating along the Heuilley canal. It is quite a heavily locked waterway and much of it is well off any beaten track; we rarely pass another pleasure boat as they mostly prefer the more touristy routes linking the north to the south. Though there are no longer any lock-keepers as such, the lock houses are the homes of people who work for the navigation authority or have done so in the past. They are mostly 'simple folk'. I'm choosing my words carefully here as I don't wish to make fun or patronise. The people we meet are so kind and generous, always pleased to chat and I know would go out of their way to help were we in trouble. Nevertheless many of them do live in a very basic fashion and, possibly due to their isolation, seem to exist in a permanent state of benign slovenliness. Cats laze in the sun while chickens peck their way in and out of the open front door. I've even seen rabbits hopping over that old fella of a dog who sleeps out on the front porch. He's the one that rouses himself, ambles over whenever he hears a boat entering the lock, and waits patiently while you ferret around for some small titbit.

Gardens are mostly well-tended and an enquiry for eggs or a lettuce will usually result in a generous wave towards the vegetable patch or a gift of green beans, tomatoes, and a few herbs. Many appear to be expressions of their owners artistic aspirations, taking the form of numerous tableaux, carefully arranged, of gnomes, plaster animals, fountains, frogs and fairies. Some of them make you smile, some make you cringe, but so what, we are just passing through and not there to make value judgements.

Anyway there we were cruising along when we came to a lock. A bit of board was propped against a stool and on it was written the one word *truffes*. 'Oh,' I say, 'they must be making homemade chocolate truffles, what a nice idea, we'll have some.' The two ladies sitting outside of the house shake their heads when I ask and a somewhat wild looking fellow comes towards us holding a box filled with several jars. These turn out to be full of real, live, preserved black truffles. The jars are of different sizes and the price for each is scrawled on the lid. Definitely nothing elegant or fancy going on here but when he unscrews the lid of one, the smell of truffle is powerful and unmistakeable. I happily pay him the price he is asking for his largest jar – it must contain at least thirty truffles and is the product of many hours of searching. I ask him where they come from and he waves his hand vaguely in the direction of the woodland behind the house. 'Do you hunt with a dog?' I ask, 'No, no … just with my eyes and nose … though I do know where to look,' he replies.

I am so pleased with our purchase. I liked the serendipity nature of it, never mind the fact that we had just netted ourselves a serious bargain. That night our lowly sausage supper was greatly elevated when paired with a dish of truffled macaroni.

I like black fungi. My best friend once found morels peppering her driveway in Somerset – she sent me a picture of them in an email asking what they were and saying her husband viewed them with suspicion and was off to the garden centre to buy some serious weedkiller. I phoned her immediately: 'No, don't do that – pick them and eat them and if you don't want to do that at least string them up over your Aga and leave them to dry. I'll take them off your hands.' We collected them in due course and they were the best dried morels we have ever had. Sadly her drive got the weedkiller treatment anyway and that was that, though I did take some sadistic pleasure in sending her vandal husband a photo I took at the market at Chalon-sur-Saône: fresh morels were selling there at 65€ a kilo!

Horns of plenty are very black indeed and for this reason I much prefer their French name – *trompettes de la mort*. They grow beneath fallen trees and dead branches which lie upon the forest floor and are often difficult to see; once uncovered though there are usually large numbers of them growing together. Although not hugely mushroomy in themselves, they can be turned into tasty dishes and always add some drama to the plate, especially when paired with something dazzlingly white. I love to mix them with black Beluga lentils, some black truffles and serve with chicken quenelles, boudin blanc or even a simply poached chicken breast.

Talking of mushrooms, I am reminded of an event which occurred a couple of years ago: we were heading down a flight of locks on the Burgundy Canal and noticed a white van driving slowly along the towpath. Every so often the vehicle stopped and the driver leapt out with a bag and squatted down in the undergrowth beside the towpath. He put something in the bag and then was off again – another few yards in the van and another stop for a squat. Strange and possibly rather private behaviour you may be thinking but he was making no effort to hide what he was about. The problem was that from the boat it wasn't easy to see just what he was up to. I got off at the next lock with the bike, caught him up and asked him what he was doing? He showed me his bag; it was full of oyster mushrooms. Hidden from us but known to him there was a line of tree stumps beside the canal. The trees had originally been planted at regular intervals alongside the towpath. Eventually, after a hundred years or more of sterling service providing shade to travellers, they had grown old and dangerous, shedding their brittle branches in the winter gales. It had been necessary to cut them down. This, according to our collector, was some years ago. Now each summer the undergrowth grew up and over them hiding them from view; beneath their damp green cover the stumps were slowly rotting away. He showed me where, around the base of each one, there grew several clumps of oyster mushrooms. Too late for me, he'd picked them all, but he generously gave me a good handful from his haul. At the next lock I jumped back onto the boat and made a quick note on the canal chart as to exactly where these treasures could be found. One day we will be back at the same time of the year, hoping to beat our white van man to it.

It has been a damp September and in the last couple of weeks we have picked several kilos of those mushrooms known as penny buns in English, *ceps* in French and *porcini* in Italian. After morels, they are tastiest ones you can find. They appear in beech and oak woods overnight and it's a bit of a battle to get to them before the slugs, deer, wild boar and other human predators. We take our chances with the hunters, usually waiting until around midday before entering the forest and leaving by 2 p.m. This is the sacred lunchtime period in France and even the hunters will be away off home tucking in to something tasty. In any event we have taken the precaution of wearing the bright yellow safety gilets that French law requires to be kept in every car, in the hope this will provide some protection against getting shot. Such are the risks a true foodie will endure!

I made a very tasty cep risotto with some of our haul but still had a huge pile left even after I had sorted them and discarded all the grotty bits. Luckily for us, a friend, who comes to find us when he judges the time is right, takes us to the woods and seems to know everything necessary about the *champignon* (witness the fact that we are still alive), arrives with a drying machine. This is a piece of kit I have never seen before but is apparently quite common in Switzerland where he comes from. It's no more than a slowly revolving fan that sits over a low-powered heating element in a container, above which are several interlocking trays with mesh bottoms. He shows me how to slice up the mushrooms and scatter them onto each tray. We pile the trays one on top of another, leaving the mushrooms to dry over the fan; every so often I check them and rearrange the trays. They slowly lose their moisture content during the course of several hours and I find that my huge pile has shrunk so much that the whole lot fits into one large Kilner jar which I proudly label with name, date and the location of the woods and canal near where they were found.

While I would never turn my nose up at shop-bought truffle sauce or commercially dried packets of morels, ceps or trompettes de la mort, there is a huge amount of satisfaction to be had from finding your own and preserving them yourself for later use. While I think it unlikely we are ever going to snuffle out our own truffles and will end up, as usual, in the Christmas market at Beaune paying mega-bucks for just one or two fresh ones, nevertheless once you get past all the hype that such items inspire, they really are quite delicious. I'm rather proud of my jars of preserves laid down in the bilges and which is now also home to my very own 'fruits of the forest'.

We decide to stop for the night above the lock at Fontenelle. There's a good mooring with strong bollards and deep water. It's there for working boats really but we haven't seen any for days. If one comes along and wants to stop he'll tie on the outside of us and be gone before we wake up in the morning. Just beyond where we have tied there's a bit of a green with a path running across towards some farm buildings. I spy a sign upon which the single word '*oeufs*' is written. 'Goody,' I think, 'easy cheese omelettes with a bit of salad for supper.' We set off in search of the chickens and sure enough, having found them and their owner, I soon have a dozen new-laid eggs in my basket.

Madame tells us she also has bottles of fresh apple juice and apple brandy for sale. They grow a lot of apples and the man with the fruit press has recently called round as he does every year. He sets it up on the little green by the canal and people come from all over with their weighty sacks of apples, pears and plums. All of madame's apples, including the windfalls, have been pressed and the resulting fermenting juice has been taken to the only distiller left in the region. He still retains the ancient rights that allow him to turn their apple juice into the heady (55% alcohol) brew known in France as eau-de-vie. Luckily for them he lives just across the green. She ushers us into his barn where she shows us the still. This is no gleaming stainless steel machine; already more than seventy years old, it is a Heath-Robinson-ish affair with a copper boiler which, when working, puffs and belches like an old steam traction engine. It is operated by its elderly owner who is known as the *'bouilleur de cru'*. Every year he hauls it out onto the green and fires it up, ready to convert everyone's fruit into alcohol. Madame explains that the juice is put into a large container like a pressure cooker at one end of the still, beneath which a wood fire burns. It takes about an hour to reach the necessary temperature for the distilling to start. Then the alchemy begins, separating the water from the alcohol. The yield, is about 10% by volume so that 100 litres of apple juice will make 10 litres of eau de vie. Madame says in a good year they usually have enough to fill one small oak barrel. She indicates the size with her hands. I think we would call it a firkin's worth – about 9 gallons. Changes in French law has seen the travelling distillers, once a common sight everywhere in France, virtually disappear. The 'grandfather rights' of the remaining few will end with their deaths. She says wryly that she hopes that their own *bouiller de cru*, a sprightly octogenarian, will last for a few years more yet.

We buy a bottle of their oldest brandy and also one of their youngest. They are very inexpensive and we are more than happy to give our support to yet another fragile thread with the past.

Later there is a knock on the side of the boat. Madame's husband is there determinedly proffering a couple of euros, because, he says, Madame has, mistakenly, overcharged us.

RECIPES

Wild mushrooms and truffles are to be found in most continental markets in the autumn but if you only have access to dried varieties of mushrooms or bottled truffles don't worry, using these in a recipe can be as good (and sometimes better) than fresh. I often use part cultivated mushrooms and part dried wild in a recipe. Here, when I talk about truffles, I am referring to the black truffle rather than the white. White Italian ones are hugely expensive and are never cooked. If you are lucky (or rich) enough to have access to any, just use them raw, thinly shaved over whatever you are putting them with. The black ones, in my opinion, are better cooked, and should be added towards the end of the cooking time. The real secret to a good truffle-y dish is generosity; don't be parsimonious with them; allow at least 10-15 grams per person.

Fresh Ceps with Chilli and Garlic

Food for the gods in my opinion and if you found the mushrooms yourself this quick, delicious and simple recipe is your reward.

For six as a starter
> *500g fresh ceps and/or chanterelles*
> *50ml olive oil*
> *a good pinch of dried chilli flakes*
> *2 garlic cloves crushed and finely chopped*
> *1 tablespoon parsley, chopped*
> *sea salt and freshly ground black pepper*

Trim the base of the ceps to remove any woody or grubby bits. Slice them lengthways into several slices. If using chanterelles, gently brush of any bits and leave whole. Don't wash mushrooms as they tend to soak up water.

Heat a few tablespoons of oil in a pan and when it's warm throw in the chilli flakes and the chopped garlic. Leave to infuse the oil for a few minutes (don't let the garlic brown), then turn up the heat and throw in the mushrooms. Cook on a medium heat for several minutes, carefully stirring them around every so often, making sure that the garlic does not burn. Add the parsley and season to taste. Place on to warm plates and serve with some nice crusty bread.

Truffled Scrambled Eggs on Toast

Try this for that special Sunday brunch. There's not a lot to it but it does taste luxurious.

For four

    12 eggs (3 per person)
    50g tin preserved black truffles
    sea salt and freshly ground black pepper
    60g butter
    1 generous tablespoon double cream or crème fraîche

Dice the truffles into 3-4 mm squares. Break the eggs into a bowl. Add the diced truffle and truffle juice. Leave covered in the refrigerator for a couple of hours. When you are ready to cook the eggs, beat them well and add some salt and pepper.

    Melt the butter in a wide shallow pan and when the butter begins to froth pour in the beaten egg and truffle mixture. Cook gently over a low to medium heat stirring all the time with a wooden spatula. Once the mixture begins to thicken, take off the heat and add the cream stirring it well to amalgamate with the eggs. Tip onto heated plates and serve immediately with a slice or two of warm and golden buttered toast.

Truffled Chicken 'en papilotte'

The big secret regarding truffles is: keep it simple – let the truffle shine. This recipe is so easy but the finished dish is ideal dinner party food.

For four

    4 free range skinless chicken breasts
    40g butter

a handful of chopped pancetta

4 medium leeks, white part only, cleaned and sliced

50g jar preserved black truffles, though fresh are better

a dash of Noilly Prat* (or other dry Vermouth)

a drizzle of concentrated chicken stock or half a stock cube

sea salt and freshly ground black pepper

4 tablespoons double cream or crème fraîche

4 squares of parchment or tinfoil big enough to loosely wrap the chicken

Preheat the oven to 180C/Gas 4

Trim the chicken breasts of any fat and sinew, bash them between two sheets of clingfilm with a rolling pin (or similar) to flatten them slightly, salt liberally on both sides, cover them and and put to one side.

Melt the butter in a pan, add the pancetta bits, cook for a minute or two, then add the sliced leeks. Sauté gently until softened – don't allow them to brown.

Peel and thinly slice the truffles. (Keep the peelings to flavour another dish). Place the 4 squares of paper or tinfoil on a baking tray and spoon some of the leeks and pancetta onto each square, scatter a few truffle slices over the leeks then top with the chicken breasts. Scatter over the rest of the truffle and and add a dash of Noilly Prat and 1 tablespoon of the cream.

Seal the package, making sure that the wrapping is fairly loose.

Place the tray in the oven and cook for about 20 minutes. Carefully open each parcel and check the chicken is done.

With a sharp knife slice the breast diagonally into several pieces.

If you want to serve the chicken *en papillote* then make sure the wrapping is resealed. Otherwise slide the chicken and its delicious truffle-y juices onto warmed plates.

I like to serve this with something really simple like some plain boiled basmati rice.

(*See My Store Cupboard Favourites, p.238)

Wild Mushroom and Potato Matafaim

This is a southern French dish and literally means 'to beat hunger' which it does spectacularly well.

For two (though it is so good that one large and hungry mouth could easily eat the lot).
250g waxy potatoes (Charlottes would be good)
50g unsalted butter
1 good size shallot chopped
150g mixed wild mushrooms, cleaned and cut into similar sized pieces
2 tablespoons fresh parsley, chopped
50g plain flour
2 eggs, separated
150ml milk
a pinch of sugar
sea salt and fresh ground black pepper
4 thin rashers of streaky bacon

Preheat the oven to 190C/Gas 5
Boil the potatoes in their skins until just tender. Drain, cool and peel, then cut into slices about 1cm thick.

Heat half the butter in an ovenproof frying pan about 20cm wide. Sauté the potato for 4 or 5 minutes on each side until golden. Remove from the pan and keep warm.

Add the rest of the butter to the pan and once it is foaming add the chopped shallot and the mushrooms. Cook over a high heat, turning them over frequently, until tender. Add half of the parsley and season to taste. Set the pan to one side.

Sift the flour into a bowl, beat in the egg yolks and milk to make a smooth batter. In a separate bowl beat the egg whites with the pinch of sugar to a snowy consistency. Fold them gently into the batter.

Return the potatoes to the mushroom pan and raise the heat. Pour the batter in, tilting the pan to allow it to run under the vegetables and spread around evenly. Transfer to the oven and cook for 8-10 minutes until fluffy and golden.

Meanwhile fry or grill the rashers until crisp.

Tear the matafaim into pieces with two forks and serve on warm plates sprinkled with the rest of the parsley and topped with the bacon.

Macaroni with Trompettes de la Mort

The original recipe was one of Michel Roux's using fresh truffles. To make the recipe more 'user-friendly' I've dropped the fresh truffle element, replacing it with a few teaspoons of Salsa Truffina* but added the trompettes de la mort for a little extra drama.

This is a very tasty dish you can make with store cupboard items if your budget does not quite stretch to fresh truffles. Were I making it with fresh then I would present it as a standalone pasta dish in an Italian influenced meal. Made with rather less elevated ingredients I find it is a perfect side-dish to pair with anything from steaks to sausages, though my personal preference is to have it with rare cooked fillets of roe deer and red wine gravy. That puts it in the special supper *'à deux'* category.

For four

> *400g large macaroni*
>
> *2 tablespoons dried trompettes de la mort*, soaked until soft in warm water then*
> *dried and finely chopped*
>
> *2 shallots, peeled and finely chopped*
>
> *1 tablespoon butter*
>
> *120g mascarpone cream*
>
> *180g dry white breadcrumbs*
>
> *2 eggs, beaten*
>
> *sea salt and freshly ground black pepper*
>
> *good pinch freshly grated nutmeg*
>
> *100g Parmesan, freshly grated*
>
> *small jar of Salsa Truffina***

Preheat the oven to 190C/Gas 5

Bring a large saucepan of water to the boil. Cook the macaroni until just al dente. Drain and set aside.

Over a gentle heat sweat the chopped shallots and trompettes de la mort in the butter in a wide shallow pan until all the moisture content has evaporated. Add the mascarpone and continue to cook for a further 3 minutes, stirring the mixture well. Take off the heat and add the breadcrumbs, beaten eggs, seasoning including the nutmeg, about half of the Parmesan and sufficient of the jar of Salsa Truffina to impart a stong truffle-y flavour. Stir everything to mix well.

Put the cooked macaroni into a lightly buttered baking dish, turning it over in the sauce until all is well coated. Sprinkle with the rest of the Parmesan and bake for 10-15 minutes until hot right through and with a golden crust on top.

(*See My Store Cupboard Favourites, p.238, ** p.239)

Velouté of Trompettes de la Mort with a Poached Egg

I have gone on rather about these little fellows. I guess because there have been a lot of them around this year. They are very good mixed in with other mushrooms. If served alone, as in the following recipe, you may need to give them a little 'taste boost' which is when a few spoonfuls of Salsa Truffina* does such a good job. I have tried to make this particular recipe using re-hydrated trompettes but it doesn't work I'm afraid; only fresh will do. Technically speaking this is not really a velouté, more of a thick 'sludge' but you probably wouldn't fancy making it if I called it that!

For four
> *50gm butter*
> *2 garlic cloves, flattened unpeeled*
> *1 small shallot, very finely chopped*
> *3-4 good handfuls of fresh, cleaned trompettes*
> *a few tablespoons of rich chicken stock (or make up140ml with concentrated*
> > *liquid stock)*
> *level teaspoonful of thickening granules**
> *Salsa Truffina to taste***
> *salt and pepper*
> *a little lemon juice*
> *4 very fresh eggs*
> *1 tablespoon chervil, chopped*
> *4 thin slices bread, to fry*

Melt the butter in a heavy-based frying pan. Add the garlic and chopped shallot and leave to cook very gently on a low gas for about 15-20 minutes.

Clean and prepare the trompettes. When the butter smells nice and garlicky, fish the garlic cloves out and add the trompettes. Turn them in the butter and cook gently until soft. I often add a tablespoon of stock to ensure they poach rather than fry.

Place the mushrooms and shallot in your food processor and reduce them to a finely chopped mixture (not a paste).

Put the mixture back in a pan, reheat, and thin down with a little more stock to a purée-like consistency. Sprinkle in the thickening granules – no more than a ½ teaspoonful – stir and cook to dissolve. By now you should have a thick dark purée. Add a teaspoon or two of Salsa Truffina. Season with salt, pepper and a few drops of lemon juice if you want. Leave the mushroom mixture in the pan and put to one side while you make the poached eggs. If this is a starter allow 1 egg per person. For a breakfast/brunch I'd make it two each.

A good poached egg needs to be very fresh. I have also found that a wok is the ideal pan for the poaching process; you can see what you are doing more readily than with a saucepan. Not being highly skilled I tend to cook the eggs two at a time and slip them, once cooked, into a bowl of cold water. When all are ready, I reheat them quickly by popping them into a pan of boiling water for a few seconds.

Fill the wok (or a wide shallow pan) with unsalted water to the depth of 10cms. Add 2 tablespoons of white wine vinegar and bring to the boil.

Break an egg gently into a small bowl or ramekin and tip it into the water at the point where it is bubbling. Repeat with the other eggs – but no more than 4 at a time max. Poach for about 1½ minutes. Using a slotted spoon, lift out the first egg and press the outside edge lightly to check that it is properly cooked. Once cooked to your liking remove with the slotted spoon and either serve immediately or transfer to a bowl of very cold water for 10 minutes. You can trim the eggs with a sharp knife and get rid of any straggly bits.

Divide the warm velouté between 4 small bowls; gently place a poached egg on top and scatter over a little chopped chervil.

Finish the dish with some quarters of crisp fried bread. A young fruity Beaujolais St Amour goes well with this.

(*See My Store Cupboard Favourites, p.235. ** p.239)

Rabbit with Mushrooms

When we worked canal boats in the UK I would make this dish using the wild rabbits caught by our lurchers. Nowadays and sadly dogless, I use French farmed ones. Whilst not quite as flavoursome as the ones we used to eat, they are always tender and more reliable to cook.

For four to six
> *750g mixed wild mushrooms (or 350g of cultivated chestnut mushrooms and a*
> > *handful of dried ceps)*
> *75g butter*
> *250g of fatty bacon, chopped*
> *1 rabbit jointed*
> *seasoned flour*
> *250g onions, chopped*
> *1 large clove of garlic, crushed*
> *200ml of Noilly Prat*, dry white wine or cider*
> *bouquet garni – small length of celery, fresh parsley, sage, thyme and a bay leaf*
> > *tied together*
> *275 ml beef stock (or concentrated bottled stock or a beef cube)*
> *parsley for garnish*

Remove any earthy bits from the mushrooms and clean with a little brush or cloth. If you have some ceps (penny buns) remove the spongy gills unless they are very young. Slice all the mushrooms. If you are using cultivated then soak a handful of dried ceps in some warm water and use these too.

Melt the butter in a pan and brown the bacon bits, then the rabbit which has been rolled in flour seasoned with sea salt and black pepper. Once the rabbit is nicely coloured remove from the pan. Add the onions and cook gently until soft-ish. Transfer everything to a casserole – preferably cast iron – with the mushrooms, garlic, bouquet garni and wine. Pour 275ml of made-up stock into the pan in which you cooked the bacon, rabbit and onion and deglaze. Add to the casserole. Add more stock and wine if necessary to cover the rabbit.

Bring gently to the boil on the top of the stove, then place in a low oven 150C/Gas 2 until cooked. This may take up to two hours if your rabbit is a wild one though rather less if it is farmed, so check it frequently; the rabbit flesh should just be coming away from the bone. Pour the stock into a separate pan and reduce to the desired flavour and consistency by boiling hard. Remove the bouquet garni. Pour the reduced stock back over the rabbit and mushrooms and garnish liberally with chopped parsley.

Serve with a really tasty mash. Ideally, steamed or boiled Charlotte potatoes put through a potato ricer. Add plenty of butter, warm milk, salt, pepper and fresh nutmeg. Beat vigorously to produce a thickish purée.

(*See My Store Cupboard Favourites, p.238)

CHAPTER 11

Mists and Mellow Fruitfulness

A ditch-crawler is by definition a bottom dweller; we like damp earthiness, mists and a little murkiness. Barging in October and November has its moments; not for everyone, I grant you, but creeping through the fog, searching for the line of canal by the tops of the trees edging the towpath and hoping not to be suddenly confronted by the bows of an empty commercial boat, so well-ballasted at the stern that there is no way its driver can see our approach, is sort of fun in a masochistic kind of way.

Rivers that in the summer are calm, sun-sparkled, boating playgrounds become dangerous maelstroms later in the year. Heavy rain and snow bring flooding with rushing waters full of hazardous flotsam. Then the boating becomes a much more grown-up deal; more fraught with danger and potential disasters and no place for a pleasure boat to be, although sometimes unavoidable. Even so the pitting of one's wits and calling upon rarely utilised skills when navigating in such conditions brings a small frisson of excitement.

We hardly see another vessel now; hire boats lose their appeal at this time of year and the rest, the privately owned cruisers and barges, are mostly tucked up in their winter moorings, engines drained, fridges emptied, their owners off to warmer climes. We occasionally pass a loaded *Freycinet* barge and exchange a few words on the radio. Otherwise we are on our own. When we tie up at night, coming in to moor above some lock far from human habitation, it is easy to be a little spooked. The vague shapes of the white Charolais cattle in the nearby fields, their bodies partly obscured by the marshy vapours creeping up around their legs, are easily transmuted into a coven of pale witches drifting slowly towards some secret destination. The screech of the heron as it finds its roost in the murky twilight is loud and harsh, the sound eerily doom laden. Later in the evening as we sit snug within our barge, books and music to hand, the slight rustling sound of something moving across the deck makes us look up, then, questioningly at each other; no, we are definitely not inclined to investigate further. During the night there's more snuffling and scratching outside and the water around and under the boat is alive with tiny agitations; it could be the pale witches stopping by to check us out. Like children we snuggle down under the duvet, covering our ears, eyes tight shut. They can't get in and we are absolutely not going out. In the morning a cat's muddy paw prints criss-crossing the deck reveals at least one culprit.

Days are short, but we start away early and tie up when it gets dark and all this barging activity makes us hungry. There's not much time for shopping nor are there many, if any, shops. Occasionally we will find a tiny weekly market of maybe a half dozen stalls set up on the defunct quay of some canal-side hamlet. Then there's a chance to stock up with a few basics: vegetables, cheese, maybe some eggs and a chicken and if we are very lucky, fresh milk poured straight from the churn into our plastic Evian bottles. Beaune market it is not, but good enough for what I need. No salads now, neither fandangles nor fol-de-rols; forget the sauces, the sorbets, the clever little starters; now we are into proper food – earthiness rules. We want pearl barley, split peas, parsnips, carrots and swedes, suet, marrow bones, ox cheeks and the emerald green cabbages of Savoy. All perfect ingredients for the long, slow cooking of stews, daubes and casseroles, their pace and timing matching our own snail-like progress along the waterway.

We spot some stalls ahead, pull in and tie to a tree. Having rapidly reconnoitred the tiny market and assessed what's on offer, I buy a plump chicken, a Reblochon cheese, swedes, chervil roots, onions, loads of spuds and half a dozen fat pork Toulouse sausages. Ten minutes later and we are, once again, on our way.

We plod steadily through a succession of locks. I am constantly up at the fore-end doing my thing. As I wait for the lock to fill I plan our lunches and dinners for the next few days; all ideally requiring the minimum of effort for the maximum return. As always this means assembling fresh tasty ingredients to start with, after that there's little more to do other than settling them over a low flame to slowly combine into a meld of mouth-watering flavours. As we leave each lock I coil the line down onto the deck ready for the next one. I lift my head, sniffing the air. Percolating up from below, the aroma of a gently simmering barley broth mingles with the faint drift of wood smoke hanging in the frosty air; the stillness only disturbed by the quiet beat of *Friesland's* heart, all of which, even were I blind, informs the other senses that we are here, boating through rural France, it is October and everyone else has left. The place, the time and the activity plus the promise of a tasty midday meal in the wheelhouse, taking turns to steer while the other eats, is as close to utter contentment as we are ever likely to find.

Next day, on waking, another typically French smell causes noses to twitch. Somewhere nearby they are harvesting a field of leeks. We decide to investigate knowing that the cropping machine always leaves behind quantities of perfect leeks and no one minds if you collect what you want before the ones left are ploughed back into the ground. Armed with a bucket and sharp knives and wearing our stout rubber sabots, we squat down in the corner of the field and create our own small harvest. There are so many that we can afford to be selective. The leeks are topped, green leaves left behind and the mud shaken from the roots; we only take the pure white stalks. Soon there's a bucketful, enough for several meals of gratins and soups, side dishes and whatever. Leeks we won't immediately use I wrap up in newspaper and leave in the bucket out on deck. At this time of year they'll happily survive for a week or more, ultimately ending up in the soup.

At the next lock the keeper comes out of his house and asks me if I would like some cooking pears? *'Bien sûr,'* I say and give him a bowl to put them in. When he returns, the bowl is empty and he hands it back to me, swiftly following it with a huge sack of pears and another of Jerusalem artichokes, freshly dug up. He looks shocked when I mention payment. Such is the plight of the ditch-crawler: one moment worrying about where the evening meal is to come from and the next, recipient of so much largesse, it's a job to decide just what to cook first.

This year we seem to have jumped into winter before we are quite ready for it. Usually there is that gentle slide through autumn doing all those nice autumn-y things: picking the last of the fruit, finishing with the quinces; watching the landscape of vines changing from green to gold; checking out the sloes and searching for mushrooms; looking to the sky and the strands of wild geese converging into the first convoys heading south. We seem to have missed all that and plunged instead into freezing fog and a finger-numbing chilliness. I mutter and shiver as I shop in the market at Langres. The stallholder serving me my onions and celeriac shakes her head – *'Le plateau de Langres, içi c'est normale.'* I think, 'Well I wish I'd known that before we slogged up fifty or so locks just to get to the bottom of this hill,' and now, having tied up at the closest point to the town from the canal, we've trudged way up here to the market in this ancient fortified citadel, which while not exactly in the clouds is, nevertheless, quite high and therefore considerably colder than the damp bottomlands where we are usually to be found. From the battlements you can see for miles and miles – or you could were it not for the aforementioned freezing fog. At least I now know why this region is called the Haute Marne.

After Langres we begin to drop down towards La Saône – lock after lock after lock – until, eventually, we turn out of the canal and into the last one before we enter the river. It is surrounded by truly magnificent, mature, plane trees and as we wait to begin our gentle descent into the free-flowing water and to our winter mooring, the golden leaves drift down with barely a whisper and settle on *Friesland's* decks.

I leave them there.

RECIPES

The following recipes are October through to February food and all the better eaten when you have been engaged in some activity outside; in our case, moving *Friesland* down through France by way of dozens of locks to her winter mooring. It's the food you want to see on the table when you come indoors stamping your feet and rubbing your hands, your nose cold and your cheeks red. Somehow it goes down better if you feel you have done something to deserve it; then one eats with gusto.

Barley Broth with Chervil Root

This is very simple peasant soup into which I have introduced the idea of chervil roots. These are small white roots with an elusive liquorice flavour. If you can't get hold of any then the best alternative is parsley root; failing those, a parsnip will do at a pinch. The soup won't taste quite the same but it's still jolly good.

For four

> 1 litre of beef stock (if you don't happen to have any to hand then Knorr
>   concentrated stock* is good or a couple of tins of beef consommé diluted)
> 14g dried ceps
> 30g butter
> 1 tablespoon cooking oil
> 1 large carrot, chopped
> 1 large onion, chopped
> 2 stalks of celery, chopped
> 5 or 6 chervil roots, cleaned and chopped
> 2 medium Charlotte potatoes, peeled and cubed
> 60g pre-soaked pearl barley
> a bay leaf or two
> 5 peppercorns
> sea salt and freshly ground black pepper
> good handful of well-chopped parsley

In a large saucepan heat the stock.

Place the ceps in a small bowl and ladle some hot stock over them. Leave to soften for around 20 minutes.

In a large shallow pan melt the butter and add the oil. Heat over a medium flame for a minute or two then add all the vegetables. Sweat the vegetables gently for about 15 minutes but do not allow them to brown. Add the soaked barley to the vegetables and cook for 5 minutes more.

Tip the vegetables into the hot stock and add the ceps and their strained soaking water. Add the bay leaf and peppercorns.

Simmer the soup in the covered pan for about an hour or until the barley is cooked. Check the seasoning and add the parsley.

Serve with chunks of fresh baked Irish soda bread and lovely salty country butter.

(*See My Store Cupboard Favourites, p.234)

Irish Soda Bread

Perfect barging bread, it takes moments to make and even fewer to eat. This is a bread without yeast which needs neither kneading nor proving. Just make sure you have some baking powder in your store cupboard.

Makes two loaves

>*500g plain flour, plus some more for dusting*
>*10g salt*
>*4teaspoons baking powder*
>*300ml thinned-down yogurt (to a thin cream)*
>*and a little oat bran (or more flour) for coating*

Preheat oven to 200C/Gas 6

In a bowl combine all the dry ingredients and mix in the yogurt to make a dough. Knead it briefly. Divide into two lumps and shape into rough rounds. Pat down to flatten to about 5 cms high. Coat all over with the oat bran or flour. Place on a baking tray and cut a deep cross into the top of each loaf. stab lightly all over with the tines of a fork.

Bake for 20-25 minutes or until the bread sounds hollow when the bottom is tapped. Cool for a few minutes on a wire rack. It is best eaten warm and well buttered.

Jerusalem Artichoke Soup and Air-dried Ham

I love the earthy, smoky taste of Jerusalem artichokes; its a shame they make you so windy. At least eating them on a barge when it's underway means you can pop out on deck and look like you are doing something useful whenever the need to let rip becomes overwhelming!

For four

> 500g artichokes
> 250g potatoes
> 1 large onion, chopped
> 1 clove garlic, crushed and chopped
> 1 stick celery, chopped
> 125g butter
> 60-80g air dried ham, chopped into small pieces
> 1 litre chicken stock
> 6 tablespoons of cream or crème fraîche
> chopped parsley and chives

Peel the artichokes and cut up into chunks. Peel and slice the potato. Put both in a large lidded pan with the onion, garlic and celery and half the butter. Cover tightly and stew over a low flame for about 10 minutes. Stir the pan occasionally. Add the ham and cook for another minute or two mixing the ham in well.

Add the hot stock and continue to simmer gently until the vegetables are all cooked right through. Allow to cool and then put through a blender. Add a little milk to dilute if necessary. When ready to serve add the rest of the butter, check the seasoning, adding more salt if required and some pepper. Just before serving stir in the cream, parsley and chives. This is quite an elegant soup in its way so a few croutons fried in butter would not go amiss.

Hearty Chicken Soup with Parsley Dumplings

There are only two items that I regularly take to France from the UK. One is my totally indispensable Maldon sea salt*, the other – a packet of Atora shredded suet*. When we are seriously into the long boating days and it's cold and dark by four in the afternoon, one begins to hanker after robust beef stews and dumplings, steak and kidney pies made with a suet-y flaky pastry and, best of all, though rarely possible, Sussex pond pudding.

On this occasion I was caught out – not enough suet left in the packet. So I made them anyway using flour, an egg and baking powder. They worked perfectly.

This is a delicious soup, hearty enough with the dumplings to have for supper; with or without, it makes a good on-board lunch too.

I usually make this soup when I have cooked chicken left over from a previous meal.

For four (with a second helping)
> *2 leeks*
> *4 carrots,*
> *2 small purple turnips*
> *2 medium waxy potatoes (ideally Charlotte or Agata)*
> *1 medium fennel bulb*
> *1 onion,*
> *2 stalks celery*
> *70g butter*
> *1 tablespoon olive oil*
> *lemon thyme, two or three big sprigs*
> *a few parsley stalks*
> *1 litre well-flavoured chicken stock*
> *750g of cooked chicken, cut into pieces*
> *2 teaspoons thickening granules**
> *salt and pepper*

For the dumplings
> *200g flour*
> *2 teaspoons baking powder*
> *1 teaspoon salt*
> *4 tablespoons Parmesan, grated*
> *4 tablespoons parsley, chopped*

1 teaspoon lemon thyme leaves, finely chopped
1 egg, beaten
about 120ml milk

Cut the leeks, carrots, turnips, potato and fennel to approximately the same size – roughly 2.5cm square. Finely chop the onion and celery and gently cook in the butter and olive oil for 5 minutes. Add the leeks and continue cooking for another 5 minutes. Add all the rest of the vegetables, turning them in the fat, and cook for another 10 minutes. Tie 2 or 3 sprigs of lemon thyme together with some parsley stalks. Add them to the vegetables and pour on the stock.

Simmer for about 20 minutes until the carrots and potatoes are just cooked.

In the meantime make the dumplings by sieving the flour into a bowl with the baking powder and salt. Add the Parmesan, parsley and thyme. Mix the egg into the dry ingredients with just enough milk to make a soft, dryish dough.

Divide into 8 balls and slide them into the soup. Cook at a robust simmer with the lid on for 12-15 minutes.

For a thicker soup add the granules. Now add the chicken and stir gently in. Give it a minute or two to warm through. Taste and adjust seasoning.

Serve in big bowls with a couple of dumplings per person. Finish with a sprinkling of parsley.

(*See My Store Cupboard Favourites, p.237)

Gratin of Leeks with Cheese

I love leeks especially at the beginning of winter when they are at their best. Don't buy huge fat ones, as thick as your average thumb is about right. This is good for lunch with just some bread, though I'm equally as likely to make it for supper when it goes very well with a couple of meaty pork sausages.

For four
    4 - 6 medium leeks, white part only
    250ml of white sauce
    200g each of Parmesan and Comté, grated
    35g butter
    100g breadcrumbs
    sea salt and freshly ground black pepper

White sauce
    25g butter
    25g plain flour
    250ml full cream milk

Prepare the leeks making sure there are no particles of grit hidden away between the leaves. Slice into 10cm lengths. Steam the leeks for 8-10 minutes. If you don't have a steamer put them in a wire sieve and steam over a pan of boiling water with a lid resting on top.

Melt the butter in a saucepan large enough to cook the sauce. Off the heat, stir in the flour and mix well making sure there are no lumps. Add a tablespoon or two of the cold milk and, again, mix well to ensure it remains lump free. Slowly add the rest of the milk whisking it all the time.

Return the pan to a low to medium heat and cook, stirring all the time, until the sauce comes to the boil. Turn the heat down and simmer the sauce gently for about 10-15 minutes to ensure that the flour is cooked. Remove from the heat and stir in about three-quarters of the cheese until melted. Taste, and season if necessary.

Remove the leeks from the steamer when cooked. Toss them gently in the butter and season well. Place them in the bottom of a shallow baking dish and pour over enough sauce to cover. Mix the breadcrumbs with the remaining cheese and scatter on top. Grill for 5 minutes under a high heat.

If you have made this in advance, to reheat and crisp the top, just pop into a preheated oven at 200C/Gas 6 for around 15-20 minutes.

Celeriac with Wild Marjoram

There is always a muddy celeriac root in the winter boater's vegetable store. It lends itself to so many meals, especially with the addition of marjoram that grows along the banks of a canal, even in November before the frosts come.

When I make this particular dish I often double the amount. The extra gets whizzed up in the blender with any leftover stock (and more water if necessary). Reheated gently it makes, topped with a liberal sprinkling of Parmesan cheese, a tasty soup for the following day's lunch.

The simple recipe here is good with almost any roast meat – lamb, steak or duck.

For four
> *700g of celeriac, trimmed into batons*
> *bay leaf*
> *400ml vegetable stock (Marigold vegetable powder* will do)*
> *2 tablespoons of marjoram leaves stripped from the stalk*
> *sea salt*
> *100ml crème fraîche*

Peel the celeriac. Cut it in half and lie each cut side down on a chopping board. Cut each piece crosswise and then cut into 1cm thick slices. Stack the slices up and cut down through them to make batons about 1cm square and around 5cm in length.

Tie the bay leaf and a couple of sprigs of thyme together with some kitchen string. Put the celeriac and herbs into a saucepan and add the stock. Bring to the boil and then reduce to a simmer until the celeriac is tender but still slightly crisp – about 8 to 10 minutes.

Meanwhile strip the leaves from the marjoram and chop well.

Once the celeriac is cooked, pour off the stock and save to use for another time leaving about 110ml in the pan. Add the cream to the pan and stir everything gently together. Cook the mixture until you have the desired result: tender strands of celeriac in a loose cream sauce. Taste and season. Stir in the reserved marjoram leaves and serve.

(*See My Store Cupboard Favourites, p.237)

Tartiflette

This is one of the great peasant dishes of France. Rich, satisfying and prone to lie a little heavily on the stomach – but who cares? For this, the true cheese to use is the Reblochon from the Savoie; though having said that I've made a pretty good tartiflette using the Maroilles cheese from the Nord-Pas de Calais region. Though not essential, and a big dish will do just as well, I like to make and serve this in individual baking dishes.

For four
> *7-8 medium waxy potatoes peeled and thinly sliced (Charlottes are perfect)*
> *50g butter*

1 tablespoon olive oil

2 large onions, thinly sliced

4 garlic cloves, finely chopped

300g smoked bacon lardons

4 good sprigs of thyme

1 glass of Noilly Prat* or dry white wine

100ml pouring cream

salt and pepper

500g Reblochon cheese (keep it cool until you use it)

Parboil the sliced potatoes until they are virtually cooked – about 7 minutes. Drain them and dry them.

In a large shallow pan melt the butter and oil, add the sliced onions and the garlic. Cook over a fairly high heat until they start to colour. Keep an eye on them as you don't want them to burn. Add the lardons and cook for another 5 minutes, turning the heat down slightly. Add the potatoes and turn the heat down further. Let everything cook gently together for about 20 minutes. Stir occasionally but gently as you don't want to break up the potatoes.

Preheat the oven 220C/Gas 7. Add the thyme, the wine and the cream, letting them warm through. Check the seasoning. Taste first because there is already quite a bit of salty bacon in there. Divide the mixture between 4 individual dishes or just use one baking dish big enough to take the lot.

Remove the rind from the Reblochon and discard. Try to work quickly with a cold knife as it can get messy if the cheese is too warm. Cut the cheese into strips and lay it over the potato mixture.

Cook in a hot oven for 20 minutes. It is ready when the cheese has mostly melted into the mixture leaving a golden crust on top.

(*See My Store Cupboard Favourites, p.238)

Pears with Griottines

If you have, at some time, made the delicious Griottines in Armagnac, (see Chapter 5, p.174), now is the perfect time to break it out from wherever you have stashed it and find out how it tastes. You could drop a couple of the griottine cherries into a champagne glass, add a dash of the, by now, richly cherry flavoured armagnac syrup they have been maturing in, and top up with some very dry champagne – assuming of course that you have everything to hand. If not, the next best thing is to buy a jar of Védrenne griottes fraîches*.

For four
> *500 ml water*
> *265g white cane sugar*
> *vanilla pod sliced vertically in two*
> *8 small firm pears peeled and halved, centres removed (Conference are good)*
> *500 ml dry white wine*
> *griottines in armagnac (or the Védrenne version)*

Bring the water, sugar and vanilla pod to a gentle simmer and when the sugar has all dissolved slip the prepared pears into the syrup. Cover with a round of greaseproof paper, with a small central hole to allow the steam to escape, cut to fit the pan. Poach the pears until they are done – anything from 15-25 minutes. Test for doneness every so often by slipping a sharp knife into the fruit. As soon as there is no resistance, the pears are done.

Cool a little and remove from the syrup. Place the pears in a bowl you can cover and refrigerate. Add a liberal amount of *griottines* and a good few spoonfuls of the liqueur. Cover and refrigerate, turning the pears gently in the cherries once or twice.

When ready to serve, remove from the fridge and taste. If the liqueur seems too powerful, add a few spoonfuls of the pear syrup until it tastes right. I must admit I quite like them strong. Serious hedonists serve the pears and cherries with vanilla ice cream and chocolate sauce but they are pretty good just on their own.

(*See My Store Cupboard Favourites, p.239)

CHAPTER 12

It's Quicker by Car

Contrary to the popular belief that the whole of France basks under a constant sun, is full of sleepy villages where buttery croissants and fresh baked baguettes are there for the taking and that the populace are charmed by our efforts to speak their language supremely badly, the truth is that many parts are subject to the same cold, rainy and blustery sort of weather that we have in the UK; the sleepy villages do exist but are so sleepy that few nowadays have a *boulangerie* – if there is any shop at all, it is, strangely, far more likely to be a hairdresser's than a baker's; as for the language thing, most natives would rather run a mile (well, a kilometre at least) than suffer the embarrassment of trying to understand the gobbledygook that the average British visitor speaks and thinks is French.

As it happens, you don't meet many French boaters on inland waters – ditch-crawling is not a French thing. This is a great shame as we know it is probably only a matter of time before the 'powers-that-be' realise that maintaining thousands of kilometres of canals and rivers for what is effectively a mere handful of foreigners is simply not a viable long term option. Without a native population of committed boaters, who will fight to save these waterways when they are at risk of closure?

Better make the most of what we have and practise our French on the few lock-keepers and lengthsmen that remain. There are some questions we always need an answer to: when does the baker's van arrive in the village we are passing through and where does it stop? If we know that and have the time to hang around we are at least assured of a fresh baguette some time during the day. The availability of all other supplies is the subject of further questioning: which day is market day or where might we find a general store or small supermarket as we boat along? The response is, often as not, the ubiquitous French shrug. As a result I always have certain items in my store cupboard that will make any number of speedy and delicious meals when there's no fresh food in sight.

Away from the busier tourist routes full of holiday-makers like the Burgundy, Nivernais and Midi Canals it is possible to spend weeks gently meandering along, stopping for days at a time in some quiet shady spot with the nearest village a good cycle ride away. This is when the store cupboard comes into its own. I invariably have a few tins of tomatoes, plenty of pasta and rice and always onions, garlic and shallots. It is also when my own stocks of wild garlic preserve, dried morels, sun-dried tomatoes, olives and goats' cheese marinated in oil take on starring roles when I'm planning the dish of the day. This being France there will always be someone, somewhere nearby, who can supply fresh eggs, a lettuce, green beans or a few raspberries and, always, parsley in abundance. The odd forage along the towpath and the surrounding countryside turns up fresh herbs and greens, often much more by way of fruit and nuts, so can also be productive. Goats mean cheese; we set off in search of a sign. If we are in cow country, a visit to the farm at milking time will generally secure a litre or two of creamy milk. In summer, simple food is all one craves. Moored far from the commercial world without easy access to butchers, bakers and candlestick-makers concentrates the mind wonderfully on producing a tasty meal with whatever is to hand. I love doing this and as a great fan of leftovers like to find ways of using up everything.

Frugal food has great appeal, at least for a while. I know I'm ready to head back towards civilisation when I start to dream of eating out in Parisian *brasseries* and see, in my mind's eye, the window displays of the more sophisticated *patisseries*.

Variety and contrast are everything: the long summer days boating through great swathes of green peacefulness juxtaposed with the charged excitement of tying up in the middle of Paris, Ghent, Amsterdam, Strasbourg or wherever; ferreting around on the canal bank for wild peppermint and oregano is, for me, (almost) as satisfying as a visit to the wonderful Paris deli, Sur les Quais which sells products from around the world; and cooking humble store-cupboard meals imaginatively is as absorbing an exercise as attempting one of those sexy recipes conjured up by some slick city chef.

It is hard to convey what this itinerant life of barging is all about and harder still to explain how very different the French that we meet en route are from us Brits; it can take several years to shed one's own preconceptions.

Recently we found ourselves back in the UK for a couple of weeks paying the price for spending a good part of the year swanning round Europe indulging ourselves. The cost? Accounts for the taxman; seeing the dentist (a lot); drastic haircuts; hacking down a jungle front and back of our small unloved terraced house and forcing ourselves to begin sorting through boxes which still lie untouched since we moved them there more than ten years ago.

You will understand therefore why an invitation from friends, excellent cooks both, to spend a long weekend at their country home in Dorset was jumped at. They had arranged a dinner for a dozen or so of their friends, most of whom we did not know. As the evening got under way, we were asked, as usual, about what we did and I said, as usual, not a lot really, though we did have a barge in France on which we moseyed about from place to place. We explain that apart from the Canal du Midi (that being the only canal that most have heard of) there is a huge waterway network covering much of the eastern and western parts of Europe and that we could boat to Brussels, Amsterdam, Paris and way beyond and never see the sea. This fact is often greeted with amazement and a certain disbelief. We explain further that it is possible to boat for thousands of kilometres on interconnected rivers and canals – into Russia, to the shores of the Mediterranean, and as far to the east as the Black Sea.

On this occasion the interest of one couple was sufficient for hubby to ask for the name of somewhere we might have stopped that he would know of, and we mention Cambrai in northern France. This was a place he recognised, albeit only as a sign about a hundred miles inland from Calais on the A26 motorway.

How long then to get to Paris from Cambrai by boat, he asked?

Captain consults his mental log and says about 44 engine hours, which is the time we actually spend on the move. If we only boated for 4 hours a day then it would take a very leisurely week and a half; being us though, it's more likely to be 4 days of almost non-stop boating.

There's a long pause as the information is assimilated.

'But you can drive to Paris from there by car, and on the motorway it only takes a couple of hours.'

His tone implies that we must be simpletons never to have realised this. Or perhaps he thinks we are part of some Amish-like diaspora whose faith commits us to forever using this odd form of outmoded transport to get around!

'Yes, we know,' we say, 'and if you include trying to find somewhere to park in Paris, it can be even quicker by train.'

But that is to completely miss the point of what we do and why we do it.

As I try to steer the conversation towards other topics, in my head I am rapidly reviewing all those brief encounters and serendipity moments which largely make up our boating experience; how the act of moving through the landscape in our leisurely way, largely unnoticed by the population on the bank, is so satisfying; the measured pace, rarely more than the speed of a fairly relaxed jogger, means there is time to take in what is going on around us, be it within the natural environment of woods and water and open meadowland or the manmade one of locks, of lifts, of tunnels, and the villages, towns and cities through which we pass.

Driving through a tunnel is nothing like boating through one and where on a motorway are you ever going to find an inclined plane?

I recall an event that had occurred in a tunnel just a few months ago. We had arrived at the entrance in time to take the afternoon tow; only one other boat was waiting – the heavily laden *Tosca* from Antwerp. The barge was moored in front of us and we walked up to talk to the Belgian skipper and his wife, principally to ask if we could go by them once we were through the tunnel. They are cheerful and accommodating and we stand around chatting, all crowded into a small patch of thin spring sunshine filtering down through the trees that shade the deep cutting. Soon after, the tug gives a hoot to let us know it is about to get underway and our little convoy sets off on its slow journey beneath the Picardy hills. We are not far from the town of St Quentin where the A26 motorway passes very nearly over the top of the tunnel. Alongside this road is one of those brown signs which indicates the presence of a nearby historic monument. In this case it is the *Souterrain de Riqueval* and the sign graphically illustrates a barge in a tunnel. We know this motorway well and each time we drive past the sign I wonder what other motorists make of it. How many of them, including the somewhat disbelieving couple we are presently talking to, realise that there are great big barges silently gliding along deep underground. Could these speeding drivers and their passengers ever begin to imagine what goes on down there? A small domestic scene, for instance, is, at this very moment, taking place beneath their wheels: the tow is well underway and Madame 'Tosca', still in her pinny, has stepped off her barge into the darkness of the tunnel towpath, hurried back along the 40 or so metres which separates our craft and handed us up a plate upon which rests two big squares of just baked, still warm, sponge cake full of juicy mirabelle plums. We thank her profusely and in the gloom of our wheelhouse proceed to scoff the lot. When, an hour or so later, we finally emerge from the tunnel, they pull over and let us go by. As we pass I lean across, hand back their plate, and wish them *'bonne route'*.

How can you compare that with a two-hour car journey speeding along a motorway, pray?

A conversation in passing from the boat to a fisherman on the bank often ends with a gift of a bucket of crayfish, a keep-net of catfish or a just found puffball. A lock-keeper hands us down some over-large courgettes from his garden as we rise in his lock. Later, when we have moored up for the night, a wander along the towpath results in a handful or two of lemony sorrel leaves; enough to turn the courgettes into a simple but delicious soup.

You won't find those in some dusty layby on your way to Paris.

What about that time when we stopped at Rethel on the Ardennes canal? Rethel – the boudin blanc capital of France where three different butchers each lay claim to its invention and vie for the title of 'Best Producer' of same. Would we have stopped there in a car? I doubt it – it being a town with very little to hold one's attention. We did though, due to some speculation in the wheelhouse as we approached the town as to which of the three might have the best credentials to support his claim. This led us to decide to stop, buy a sausage from each of the claimants and judge the one we thought was best for ourselves. Boudin blanc is an inoffensive sort of thing, mild in taste and somewhat anaemic looking with its pale intestinal skin and minced chicken interior. Some might think it rather bland but it makes a tasty enough supper teamed with some onion gravy and mash; spectacularly good too sliced, with tagliatelle and a truffle sauce.

We walked into the town, purchased the first two, one from each butcher, and then entered the third and final shop. Our sausage chosen and wrapped, we passed over the cash. As I went to take it from its maker he suddenly withdrew his hand (and the sausage) and said in a slightly accusatory tone, 'Are you English?' 'Yes we are,' we shyly admitted, thinking he was about to thank us for our good work during two world wars. Not a bit of it. 'As you are English and therefore cannot cook it is necessary for me first to explain to you how to prepare this boudin blanc.' I made a small noise of protest and a half-hearted grab for it. He held it tightly to his chest. 'You must first heat a little butter in a pan and cook it, oh so gently, so as to just heat it through and lightly colour the skin – no more than twelve minutes in total.' I nod in what I hope he will take to be knowledgeable agreement and he proffers the package. I go to take it but it is once again withdrawn. 'Madame,' he looks at me sternly, 'you must be most patient when you cook it. If the heat is too high you will burn the butter and cause the sausage to split. This must not happen.' 'No, no,' I say, 'it won't.' He holds out for a moment longer and then with obvious reluctance hands it over. We leave quickly in case he should change his mind.

You may laugh, but this is not your average 'take it or leave it' supermarket transaction. French shopkeepers see themselves as trained professionals and are often running a business that has been passed down through several generations; it's best not to argue. Twice before in France we have been refused something on display that we wanted to buy. Once in Paris when I was looking for mushrooms for that evening's meal, we came across a small greengrocer's. The interior was dark and the patron, an elderly man in a long brown coat, taciturn. I bought the mushrooms but then spotted a tray of apricots on the counter. There they sat, golden and glowing, lighting up the shadows like so many miniature suns. In my best French I asked for, *'Un livre des abricots, s'il-vous plaît, monsieur.'* *'Non,'* came the reply, 'they are not yet ready – if you want some you must return two days from now.' With that he turned his back, the conversation over. Another time in the *fromagerie* in Chalons-en-Champagne, Madame Husson refused to sell me a Langres cheese. 'Come back in a week – it will be ready for you then.' 'But can't I take it and keep it until then?' 'Of course not,' she tells me, 'you cannot possibly have the right conditions in your home to ripen this cheese and what do you know about cheese anyway?' Humbled, I back off and duly return on the appointed day to collect the cheese, which by now had been brought to the appropriate state of perfection. That evening, with a little marc de champagne poured into the depression in the top, and a handful of grapes, it rounded off our meal a treat.

As I recall, in the case of the boudins blanc, they all tasted much the same but to my mind butcher No.3 was the obvious winner. In spite of calling us rotten cooks he clearly felt a responsibility to ensure that his little sausage, even in the hands of Philistines, received the appreciation it deserved.

And what about some of the really grotty places that canals go through, the old industrial centres that they were originally built to serve, now deserted, left to the graffiti artists and scrap metal men? It is not unusual to stop on a defunct commercial quay and pick our way out through the shards of glass from broken-windowed factories or cross an abandoned aggregates wharf to squeeze through the disintegrating fence onto the road. No passing car is ever likely to stop to explore here, but we do, and will likely be rewarded with a family restaurant in the rundown town, often the enterprise of immigrant Greeks, Italians or Turks shipped in to do the local dirty work more than a generation ago. The industry they came to serve has long departed, but they are still there and still to be found cooking up the authentic dishes of their homelands to an appreciative community, and to us.

When I think of all the people we have encountered on our travels, those fleeting interactions, the meetings and departures, the easy sharing of common ground, I find it hard to imagine any other circumstances where such events could occur. So we count our blessings and hug our barging life to ourselves.

Our Dorset friends hand round small squares of warm Tarte Maroilles with the apéritifs. We have brought them a gift of these very special tarts from northern France. The 'speedy car' people exclaim over their deliciousness and are off again – 'What is this?', 'Where do you get it from?', 'What sort of cheese is this?' 'Did you make it yourself?' etcetera, etcetera. We say that we often moor up on the canal near the farm where the cheese tarts are baked each day by the farmer's wife and sold in their shop. She vacuum-packs them, we buy them to have for lunch, and also to bring back to England to share with friends.

The 'quicker by car' couple want to know the address, asking for directions on how to find the farm.

Sadly, we can't be of any help, as we only know how to get there by boat.

RECIPES

These are real 'ditch crawler' recipes and are usually the result of seizing the moment. If a fisherman offers me a huge catfish he's just dragged out the Saône, I for one would not refuse it though this is a most alarming looking creature and best beheaded as quickly as possible. It is also an intensely slippery character and even when dead feels as though it is still wriggling under your hand as you start to fillet it. We have eaten catfish in France and Serbia and they are hugely popular in the southern states of the USA. They are a white firm-fleshed, mild tasting river fish. I normally just fillet them and panfry.

Crayfish caught in clean river water or high up on the summit of a canal are delicious. In the UK we now have a problem with the signal crayfish, which is overwhelming our native species. This is a sad state of affairs but the signals taste just as good as our home-grown variety so why not do your bit for the environment by catching and eating them – but best to avoid those which lurk in waterways in towns and cities. In France you can buy crayfish traps though we used to catch them with just a bit of bacon tied on the end of some string. They like rotten meat best; if you have none to hand apparently a punctured can of dog food will attract their attention!

As a keen advocate of towpath foraging it is rare during the Summer months not to be able to find plenty of sorrel along the canal bank. It is so common that by keeping a sharp lookout almost anywhere you happen to be, your reward will be a harvest of these lemony leaves.

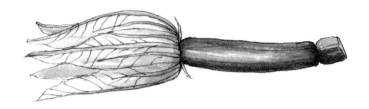

Courgette and Sorrel Soup

For six

> *50g butter*
> *2 shallots, finely diced*
> *900g courgettes chopped*
> *1¾ litres chicken stock*
> *2 good handfuls of sorrel, washed and shredded*
> *1 cooked waxy potato cut small (or enough potato flakes to thicken the soup)*
> *salt and pepper*
> *crème fraîche to garnish*

In a good sized pan soften the butter and sweat the shallots until they are transparent – don't let them brown. Stir in the chopped courgettes, mix well with the butter, cover and cook gently for about 10 minutes. Add enough chicken stock to cover the vegetables. Bring to the boil, turn down the heat and simmer until the courgettes are just cooked. Add the sorrel and let it melt down into the courgettes. Liquidise the soup and pour into a clean pan. Leave to cool for a moment while you purée the potato separately using a potato ricer. Add the potato and mix in well. (If you prefer to use potato flakes then sprinkle enough into the liquid to thicken it and stir well). If the soup is too thick add more stock. Taste and season.

To serve, pour into bowls, add a swirl of crème fraîche and a garnish of fresh chopped sorrel leaves.

(I often use *Maggi Natural Mashed Potato Flakes as the the thickening agent instead of the fresh potato – see My Store Cupboard Favourites, p.236)

Crayfish Soup

There is a whole lot of work involved in making this soup but it is so worth it. I must admit to cheating slightly as I have never managed to catch more than a couple of crayfish myself, though I did once acquire a whole load from a man fishing them out of the river fed Canal St Quentin. The ones for this recipe I bought from a glorious fish stall in the Halles Paul Bocuse market at Lyon.

For four to six
>   *1kg of live crayfish*
>   *50ml olive oil*
>   *6 cloves of garlic, crushed and peeled*
>   *2 medium bulbs of fennel, roughly chopped*
>   *3 sticks of celery, roughly chopped*
>   *1 largish carrot, roughly chopped*
>   *1 large white onion, well chopped*
>   *a good pinch of saffron pounded in a drop of hot water*
>   *400g chopped plum tomatoes*
>   *1 tablespoon semi-dried tomatoes, puréed*
>   *85ml dry white wine*
>   *1 litre fish stock*
>   *juice ½ lemon*
>   *salt and freshly ground black pepper*
>   *a glug of pastis*
>   *a glug of Cognac*

Leave the crayfish under a tap of running water for 5 minutes to wash out any muddy particles. Place them in a freezer for an hour to dull their senses. You will need a large saucepan full of boiling water in which to cook the crayfish. Cook them in batches for about 10 minutes, then fish them out and plunge into very cold water.

Once they are all cooked and cooled, remove heads, carapace, claws and tails. Discard the heads, which have a rather muddy flavour. In a large casserole heat the olive oil over a medium heat. Throw in the garlic, fennel, celery, carrot and onion and sweat gently for about 20 minutes with the lid on, stirring the pot occasionally; don't let anything brown. Add the saffron, the tin of tomatoes and the tomato purée, the wine, the claws and tails and all the meat plus the fish stock and cook for a further 20 minutes.

Using either a powerful hand blender or food processor, crunch everything up finely. Then strain the lot into a second container, through a couple of layers of wet muslin placed in a sieve. It's a bit of a messy process (do it for your art!); finish with a really good squeeze of the muslin. You should end up with a clear, saffron-coloured liquor.

Pour the liquid into a pan, place over a medium heat, uncovered and simmer until it is reduced by half. Add the lemon juice and season carefully until you have a rich and tasty broth. Add the Pastis and Cognac and heat for a minute or two longer to cook off the alcohol.

Serve with toasted rounds of *ficelle* (a thin version of a baguette), a home-made garlicky chilli mayonnaise and a bowl of grated Parmesan to sprinkle on top.

Jane Grigson in her book *Good Things* supplies a couple of useful recipes for the mayonnaise.

Recipe One: In a mortar, pound 2 plump cloves of garlic and the flesh of 2 fresh red chillies with a little salt. Soak a thickish slice of white bread in a drop of fish stock. Squeeze it well and add to the mortar. Stir in little by little 3 tablespoons of olive oil and some fish stock until you have the right consistency.

Recipe Two: In a mortar pound three plump cloves of garlic with the flesh of 2 chillies. Beat in two egg yolks. Gradually add 220ml mix of half olive oil and half grape seed oil. Finish by stirring in a little Dijon mustard, salt and pepper to taste.

I find a teaspoon or two of sun-dried tomato purée is a good addition to either of these recipes.

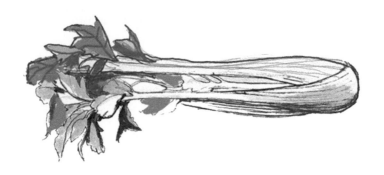

Catfish Chowder with Comté Cheese

For four

 20g butter
 ½ small onion, chopped
 200ml chicken stock
 125ml water
 30g celery, chopped
 70g baby carrots, sliced
 1 large potato, peeled and cubed
 380ml milk
 25g plain flour
 ½ teaspoon celery salt
 1 teaspoon ground cumin
 Maldon sea salt and fresh ground black pepper to taste
 350g catfish fillets, cut into 2.5cm pieces

85g Comté cheese, grated
1 tablespoon parsley, freshly chopped

In a large saucepan over a medium heat, melt the butter and sauté the onion until tender. Pour in the chicken stock and water. Mix in the celery, carrots and potato. Cook for around 15 minutes, stirring occasionally, until the vegetables are tender.

In a small bowl, whisk together 170ml of the milk and the flour making sure it is lump free. Pour into the saucepan of vegetables and stock, stirring all the time.

Add the remaining milk, celery salt, cumin, and season to taste. Stirring occasionally, continue cooking the mixture for about 10 minutes, until it has thickened.

Add the catfish morsels and cook for a further 5 minutes or until fish is easily flaked with a fork. Gently stir in the cheese until it has melted into the soup.

Serve in bowls with the parsley scattered over the top.

Panfried Catfish in Cornmeal

For four
oil for frying
200ml milk
100g fine cornmeal
1 teaspoonful sweet smoky paprika
½ teaspoonful cayenne
¼ teaspoonful celery seed
4-6 catfish fillets (more if they are small)
sea salt and freshly ground black pepper
a good handful of watercress for each plate – thick stalks removed
1 lemon, quartered

Have the oven on very low, just to keep the fillets warm as you cook.

Heat 2 tablespoons of oil in a frying pan.

Pour the milk into a shallow dish.

Mix the cornmeal, paprika, cayenne pepper and celery seed together and put into another shallow dish.

Moisten each catfish fillet in the milk, remove and season with salt and pepper. When the oil is hot enough, dredge the fillets in the cornmeal mix, making sure that each side is well covered. Shake off any excess and gently place in the hot oil. Fry until golden brown for anything from 2-4 minutes – depending upon the thickness of the fillet.

As they cook remove them to the oven onto a wire rack placed over an oven tray while you do the rest.

Serve with watercress and a lemon quarter

(This is a generic recipe in that you can use almost any thinnish white fish fillets instead of the catfish, or even flattened chicken breasts escalopes.)

Boudin Blanc with a Cep and Truffle Sauce and Tagliatelle

I cook the boudin blanc the way the maker specified: in butter, very gently to achieve a nice golden tan. This takes around 10-15 minutes and is not to be rushed or the skin will split. This would be the ultimate sin in the world of boudin blanc aficionados.

It is a real cheat's dish but does mean that one can put together an elegant little supper in no time at all.

For two
enough tagliatelle for two
knob of butter
2-3 boudin blanc sausage
50g butter
40g of Salsa Truffina or similar*
a little Knorr concentrated chicken stock**
110ml double cream

This is so quick, though you do need to be dealing with all three of the elements more or less simultaneously. I tend to start with the cooking of the tagliatelle, draining it when it is at the al dente stage, but leaving it in a little cold water while it's waiting to prevent the pasta from sticking together. Immediately before serving, I drain off the cold and pour over enough boiling water to just cover the pasta. One minute on a high heat will reheat the pasta without overcooking it. Drain the boiling water and add a small knob of butter. Keeping it on the heat, turn the tagliatelle gently in the butter, making sure all the water has evaporated.

While the pasta is cooking, gently fry the boudin blanc in butter until the outside is nicely coloured.

Remove to a warm oven.

225

Empty the contents of the jar of Salsa Truffina into a small pan. Add a drop of concentrated chicken stock and a couple of tablespoons of water. Mix well and place over a gentle heat. Add the cream and cook to the required viscosity for the sauce to coat the tagliatelle.

To serve: place a boudin blanc on a warm plate and slice it into five or six slices. Put a small pile of tagliatelle beside it and spoon over the truffle cream sauce. When they are available I sometimes add a handful of girolle mushrooms to the pan in which the boudin blanc was cooked. Fry them quickly and garnish each plate with a few of them.

(*See My Store Cupboard Favourites, p.239, ** p.234)

Boudin Blanc with Garlic and Onion Purée and a Spring Onion Mash

Garlic cooked to a delicious purée loses its brashness and becomes soft, sweet and beguiling. The amount of purée this recipe makes is rather more than is needed for a meal for two but it stores well and lends itself to all sorts of other dishes. I like it spread on toast eaten with a poached egg for a speedy snack or light lunch.

For two

> 2-3 *boudin blanc sausage*
>
> 1 *tablespoon flat-leaf parsley, finely chopped*

Garlic and Onion Purée

> 3 *whole heads of garlic*
>
> 350g *onion, roughly chopped*
>
> 8 *tablespoons olive oil*
>
> *Maldon sea salt*

Spring Onion Mash

> 650g *peeled potatoes, preferably Charlotte*
>
> 150ml *warm full-fat milk*
>
> 50g *butter*
>
> *bunch of spring onions, chopped*
>
> *Maldon sea salt and freshly ground black pepper*

Make the onion and garlic purée first. Separate the cloves garlic but do not peel. Place in a heavy-based pan with the onion and olive oil. Cover and stew very gently over a low heat until both garlic and onion are meltingly tender – a good 40 minutes or more. Leave the mixture to cool slightly. Using your hands, squeeze the cooked garlic out of its skin, liquidise the onions and garlic together, taste and season.

Reheat when ready to serve.

Meanwhile cook the potatoes in plenty of salt water. When cooked, drain and dry off. Mash them with plenty of creamy milk and butter (do not liquidise as it makes them taste glue-y). Keeping the allium theme going and to give the potatoes some substance add about 6-8 chopped spring onions to the mash. Season with salt and pepper. Stir well.

Cook the boudin blanc as above. Remove to a warm oven until ready to serve.

Put the boudin blanc and mash on warm plates. Pour over some of the garlic and onion purée and scatter with the parsley.

Mirabelle Plum Sponge Pudding

This filling fruity plateful is a great autumn dessert especially as you can make it with almost any seasonal fruit that you can get your hands on. Sometimes it's known as an 'upsidedown' pudding or when made with apples, 'Eve's pudding'. Although it was fed to us by a Belgian barge lady in a French tunnel it has been a stalwart of the English kitchen, probably since ovens were first invented.

For four to six
450g Mirabelle plums
75g light soft brown sugar
100g butter, plus extra for greasing
100g caster sugar, plus extra for sprinkling
2 eggs
100 g self-raising flour
½ teaspoon vanilla essence

Wash and dry the plums and spread them over the base of a buttered ovenware dish so they lie closely together in one layer. Sprinkle with the brown sugar. Mix the fruit and sugar lightly together. Cream the butter and caster sugar. Work in the eggs, sifted flour and vanilla essence and mix to a soft batter. Spread over the plums. Bake in a preheated oven at 180C/ Gas 4 for 40 minutes. Sprinkle the surface with caster sugar.

Best served warm in wedges with cream or custard.

N.B. I leave in the stones but warn guests of their presence.

Tarte Maroilles

In spite of the 'speedy couple' I have decided to relent and share the recipe for this brilliant tart. Maroilles cheese is, deservedly, one of the great cheeses of France but, being extremely smelly, does not travel well. The dough mix seems to be a particular feature of Flemish baking and is quite similar to another regional speciality – *Tarte au Sucre.*

> *250g Maroilles cheese*
> *1-2 tablespoons liquid crème fraîche (or single cream)*
> *freshly ground black pepper*

Dough
> *5g fresh baker's yeast*
> *75g warm milk – no hotter than 30C*
> *1 level teaspoon caster sugar*
> *250g French T55 flour (or equivalent strong bread flour)*
> *½ teaspoon fine salt*
> *3 medium eggs, lightly beaten*
> *50g butter, melted*

Make the dough: begin by dissolving the fresh yeast in warm milk with the sugar. Stir gently.

In a large bowl, mix the flour and the salt. Make a well in the centre and pour in the eggs and the yeast mix.

Start mixing from the centre drawing the flour in from the edges of the bowl. Once well mixed, beat the dough vigorously for 10 to 15 minutes to incorporate the maximum amount of air. Add the melted butter still stirring briskly. The dough must be very soft, almost liquid.

Butter and flour a circular baking tin about 23cm in diameter. You will need 250g of dough for the base of one tart. Put the dough in the tin, sprinkle flour lightly over the top, then using the palm of the hand spread the dough all over the base to about 5cm in depth.

Leave the orange crust on the cheese and cut into thin slices. Spread the slices all over the dough so they make one layer. Brush 1-2 tablespoons of crème fraîche over the cheese and give a couple of twists of the peppermill. Leave, covered, to rest, away from draughts, for another hour. The dough will increase in volume.

Preheat the oven to 200C/Gas 6.

Bake for around 40 minutes or until the cheese is browned and the dough is crisp.

Serve warm with a green salad or a dish of baked tomatoes.

MY STORE CUPBOARD FAVOURITES

For several years, whilst wandering the waterways of France, Belgium and Holland, I wrote a 'foodie/barging' blog. It was aimed, primarily, at others who were doing much the same thing, so I did not give too much thought to how a wider audience might obtain the various ingredients I mentioned in passing. I am pleased to say that it is still not quite possible to buy exactly the same products in every country one visits. In spite of incipient globalisation many still cleave to their own particular cuisines and the ingredients thereof; in any case some foods just don't travel.

'My Store Cupboard Favourites' is compiled partly in recognition of this though it also lists those items that I, as a committed 'foodie', need in order to produce meals beyond the basic. Space in a barge's larder is limited and when one is mostly on the move it needs to be filled with only those items the cook can't easily live without.

Like most people I often make use of readily available products rather than construct a whole dish from scratch. I have a list of what I call my secret ingredients, which means when friends come to dinner and compliment me on my food, I don't usually broadcast the fact that I may have used instant thickening granules instead of making a proper *beurre manié*, or that my deeply flavoured mushroom sauce owes more to a tin of wild mushroom powder than to ceps freshly gathered from the forest that morning. Such products provide useful shortcuts in cooking. They range from the boringly mundane to the slightly esoteric but all are useful things to have in the store.

Some of the products on my list are not particularly unusual; some are easy to find in a French supermarket, more difficult to locate in the UK and vice versa. Other items are there because they are included in a particular recipe or because I think their properties and the different ways of using them could be better known.

Nowadays most items, wherever they come from, can be located via the internet and I list below one or two favourite sites of my own.

Atora Beef Shredded Suet

Who could survive without a packet of Atora in their cupboard – especially barging in France? There is no French equivalent product and I can find no history of them using suet for baking. For me winter beef stew is incomplete without dumplings and I have to make at least one bacon pudding a year. Easy to buy in the UK I always take a packet with me.

Black Garlic

This adds real depth of flavour to even the most prosaic of casseroles and makes an interesting little sauce-cum-gravy for chops, steaks and even beefburgers or sausages. Though it looks a bit yukky, being nothing more than very old garlic, it is really good. Hard to find other than on the Internet but as it seems to last forever unopened, it's worth getting a few packets at a time. There are loads of recipes to stimulate your interest and where to buy it on the web-site www.blackgarlic.co.uk

Bonne Maman Oranges Amères

Easily found in France and nowadays available in the UK where it is called bitter orange marmalade. This particular product is more like a slightly sharp, very fruity orange confit, rather than a proper jam or marmalade. Although delicious in its own right spread on toasted brioche, I use it, among other things, as the base for my orange butter sauce. This sauce works really well with asparagus, shell fish, artichokes and green beans.

Canadou Sucre de Canne Liquide

Add this to your French supermarket trolley. You will find it somewhere on the shelves where they keep the rums and various fruit-flavoured eau-de-vies. Straightforward sugar cane syrup, it is usually used to make cocktails and the exotic apéritifs the French are so fond of and which I certainly would not say no to. It is what I use on any fresh fruit salad that benefits from a little extra sweetness. Add it little by little as it is intensely sweet.

Duck Confit

A wonderful product made by many companies in France. When I'm there I often buy the artisan made confit in jars from farms or markets. I bring it back with me when I return to England. More usually good quality confit can be found in big round flat tins on French supermarket shelves. Google it to buy in the UK. Waitrose sell it online and there are several specialist sellers of British made. The French label Lamaudie is available from Amazon.

Figaro Mesquite Liquid Smoke

This is an American product that is meant to add flavour to barbecued meat. I have never tried doing this. I do add it to almost any casserole or sauce that I think will be enhanced by the wonderful smokiness it imparts. Obvious candidates are beefy stews but anything faintly Spanish using red peppers and paprika benefits from a few drops, as does a red wine gravy. A little goes a long way. Buy it and try it.

It occasionally turns up in specialist food shops in the UK but you can go to www.figaroco.com to find stockists.

Guérande Fleur de Sel

This is the best salt to use on roasted marrow bones or with pâté de foie gras. It doesn't need grinding. It is harder than Maldon sea salt and has a subtly different taste. Nowadays it is easy to find in UK supermarkets and online.

Knorr Jus de Roti

I don't know why you can't get these stock cubes in the UK but I have only ever seen them in French supermarkets. You will find them on the shelves where all the jars of herbs and spices live. Use one to increase and enhance your gravy. I often crumble about half a cube into the roasting tin, pour in some wine, let it reduce a bit, add water and stir well. Reduce again if it needs a stronger flavour or add the rest of the cube if you want more gravy.

Knorr Concentrated Stock

The reverse is true of these useful little bottles of concentrated stock. Easy to find in any UK supermarket but not used at all in France. I always have one of beef and one of chicken in my store cupboard. Invaluable for making an instant stock but even more useful, being in liquid form, a dash can be added directly to whatever I'm cooking to give it a boost of flavour. I often add a spoonful to a wine reduction when making a sauce or to soups, casseroles and other meat dishes.

Leonardi's Caramelised Figs in Balsamic Vinegar

On its own this is absolutely stunning with a slice of pâté de foie gras and some toasted brioche. I thin it down with a drop of water and some olive oil to make the dressing for my Asparagus with Figgy Balsamic. I use it to dress beef carpaccio and as a savoury counterpoint to a dish of Piel de Sapo melon, fresh figs and Parma ham. Get some and you will soon find yourself using it in no end of different ways.

Track it down at www.acetaialeonardi.it

Leonardi's Saba Dressing

This is a condiment made from slow cooked grape must aged in barrels. It is the basis of balsamic vinegar. In this form it is hauntingly, sweetly reminiscent of a rich dessert wine. Saba has been around since Roman times and can be used in a variety of foods both sweet and savoury. Leonardi's is quite expensive, though a little goes a long way. You can find cheaper versions – I have a little bottle of something called Vincotto that works very well. Track it down by googling Saba/Vincotto condiment or go to Leonardi's website: www.acetaialeonardi.it

A L'Olivier Aged Balsamic Vinegar

This is the best balsamic on the market in my opinion. Along with their delightful fruit flavoured vinegars and condiments I rate A L'Olivier products very highly.

I really enjoy my annual forage at one of the A L'Olivier shops in Paris, Lille, Lyon or Strasbourg – all cities which are easily accessible by barge. However, if you are UK based they do now have a London shop at: 15 Kensington Church St, W8. Tel: 020 7937 5114 or email: info@alolivier.co.uk. You can also find some of their range on Amazon.

McDougalls Thickening Granules

This product is definitely not a French thing, so if you are barging about in France you will need to bring it with you from the UK. Easily found in most big supermarkets near the flour and baking stuff, it is nothing more than a thickening agent; a mixture of cornflour and vegetable oil that has been processed into granules. Unlike some of the old-fashioned thickening products, it is tasteless and colourless. I use it instead of a *beurre manié* and add it towards the end of the cooking process. Because the granules dissolve quickly, it is easy to add a little at a time until the right density is achieved. I use it if I want to thicken a gravy or sauce and often when I'm adding cream or crème fraîche to a sauce as it seems to make it more stable. It is stocked by all the popular supermarkets.

Maggi Mashed Potato Flakes

This is so useful – especially in soups. I find potatoes whizzed up in a blender tend to have a gluey taste. For a quick lunchtime soup I use the Maggi flakes instead. The required amount can just be mixed into the finished soup. I have used them on one or two occasions to make a very acceptable instant mash. Easily found in any French supermarket. In the UK I think it would be necessary to order from the Maggi website.

Maille Mayonnaise

This is found in the refrigerated section near the butter and cream in most French supermarkets. Made by Maille, a company best known for its Dijon mustard, it is quite mustardy for a mayo. Depending upon how I am intending to use it, I will thin it down a bit with cream or Greek yoghurt to soften the flavour, or mix it with other ingredients or do a bit of both. Please note this is not a substitute for real home made mayonnaise that you intend to use on its own, but is excellent as the base for many mayo-type dressings. I often add it to my own standard salad dressing for certain dishes like an asparagus and smoked salmon salad.

A jar of Maille mayonaise will live happily unopened in the fridge for ages, and even, once opened, will keep for several weeks.

Maille Mustard

Although the standard Dijon is easy to find in supermarkets both in the UK and France, the product I prefer, especially when adding to sauces or salad dressings, is the Maille Moutarde Mi-Forte, which is a milder, less acidic mustard. This, I have only been able to buy in France. It can be found with several other specialist French items at www.frenchclick.com

Maldon Sea Salt

Who could live without it? I take it everywhere I go. Easily bought in Britain but hard to find wandering through Europe on a boat. Makes a great present to give to foreign foodies too. Now that it is so popular it is easily sourced on the web.

Marigold Vegetable Stock Powder

Like the commercial concentrated fish and meat stocks this vegetable powder is such a useful item, lending itself to the making of instant soups and adding a depth of flavour to many dishes. Easily found in the UK though not a common product in France.

Merchant Gourmet precooked products

I love Puy lentils and often cook them from scratch but it's always worth having a few sachets of Merchant Gourmet's various precooked lentils and rice in your store cupboard. They lend themselves to so many things and are the basis for many soups and salads. You can serve them, suitably flavoured, as a side dish for both fish and meat based meals and are ideal veggie food. Useful too for a quickly prepared meal after an overlong apéritif hour with friends. I buy them in Waitrose when I'm in the UK, otherwise you can order Merchant Gourmet products from their website at www.merchantgourmet.com

Mushrooms, dried

Morels reconstitute beautifully and are very flavoursome. Dried ceps give a depth of flavour to all sorts of soups and casseroles while the blackness of trompettes de la mort adds a touch of drama to any number of dishes. These are standard items to be found in France in both supermarkets and from specialist shops. If you can't bring them back from France then a search of the internet should throw up plenty of suppliers.

Noilly Prat

I've never drunk this as an apéro except once when moored where this old-fashioned vermouth is made in Marseillan, in the south of France. It is easily found among the ports, sherries and other fortified wines on supermarket shelves in both France and the UK. It is the base for virtually every pale sauce or gravy I make. A few fine chopped shallots and a slosh of Noilly Prat reduced down to little more than a teaspoonful is the classic start to many sauces. I much prefer it to white wine for that initial reduction; its slightly bitter herbiness seems to have more punch and is better at bringing the various elements of the sauce together.

Panzani Sauce Tomate

I have never seen this product in the UK but it is easily found in any French supermarket. It is so useful I always bring several tubes with me back to the UK. You can use it like tomato purée but is far less acidic than the normal ones as it is made with the addition of other vegetables. I use it in any number of recipes – soups, sauces, casseroles, ratatouille, whatever. You can even make the quickest sauce ever for pasta. Squirt a couple of tablespoons worth into a small saucepan, thin down with a little water, add some double cream or crème fraîche, whisk all together whilst heating gently. Pour over fresh pasta. Serve with some Parmesan. It is quicker to make than it is to write the recipe!

Salsa Truffina

This is a great little jar of mushroom purée strongly flavoured with truffles. A couple of teaspoons mixed into almost dish made with mushrooms will really make it zing. Do this at the end of the cooking so you don't lose the truffle flavour. Add it to a creamy mushroom sauce to top some pasta or stir it into a mushroom risotto. I add a little to my mushroom fricassée, to my velouté of trompettes de la mort or even an omelette. It will perk up any dish made with plain old shop bought mushrooms. It keeps for several weeks in the fridge once opened.

This is a product that both Waitrose and Sainsbury's sometimes sell. I have never seen it on sale in France. You can find stockists or order it on line at www.laquila.co.uk

Shake o'Cini wild mushroom powder

Despite its silly name this is an exceptionally good product. Not only does it increase the depth of flavour of any mushroom dish you may be making, especially if the only ones to hand are the common old white ones, and added to beefy casseroles and meat-based sauces like bolognaise, it gives an added intensity to the dish.

It can be tracked down on the Internet. Try the excellent Sous Chef website – https://www.souschef.co.uk/

Védrenne Supercassis and Crème de Mûre

Beyond just being the basis for the delicious apéritif Kir there are so many puddings which are greatly enhanced with a quick splash of one of Védrenne's many fruit liqueurs. I love a tablespoon or two of Crème de Myrtille on blueberries when I make a blueberry crumble. I add Crème de Mûre to the juice in which I soak the bread casing of a Summer Pudding. A dash of Supercassis can enhance a sauce or gravy for calves' liver or pigeon breasts or blackcurrant jelly. Buy Védrenne – it's the best and not too expensive; don't go for the fancy bottles; they tend to cost more. Go to www.vedrenne.fr to order though it is far better to call in at their showroom at Nuits St Georges in Burgundy if you happen to be passing.

Useful General Websites

If you are a keen cook the website https://www.souschef.co.uk is very good for buying slightly obscure items that you can't readily get your hands on.

For all things French try https://www.frenchclick.co.uk.

Cream in France

When cooking in France (where British double, single and whipping cream are rarely to be found), or simply following a recipe which calls for crème fraîche, check the butterfat content of the product you are using. Generally speaking the higher the butterfat content (between 35% and 45%) the less likely the cream will be to split at high temperatures as long as it is initially brought to the boil slowly and gently. Crème fraîche and double cream can be used interchangeably in cooking, and both are equally good for baking.

Crème fleurette and crème liquide have a similar consistency to whipping cream. When very fresh both are quite runny and without the sharper taste of crème fraîche. Perfect for dishes requiring slow simmering and as long as the fat content is 30% to 35% will not separate even when brought to boiling point.

BIBLIOGRAPHY

Lindsey Bareham: *A Celebration Of Soup*
Publisher: Penguin 1993

Sally Clarke: *Sally Clarke's Book*
Publisher: Grubb Street 2004

Gennaro Contaldo: *Passione*
Publisher: Headline Book Publishing 1993

Margaret Costa: *Four Seasons Cookery Book*
Publisher: Papermac 1970

Skye Gingell: *A Year in My Kitchen*
Publisher: Quadrille Publishing Ltd 2006

Peter Graham: *Mourjou*
Publisher: Prospect Books 2004

Jane Grigson: *Good Things*
Publisher: Penguin 1971

Jane Grigson: *Jane Grigson's Fruit Book*
Publisher: Penguin 1982

Amanda Hesser: *The Cook and the Gardener*
Publisher: Absolute Press 1990

Simon Hopkinson and Lindsay Bareham: *Roast Chicken and Other Stories*
Publisher: MacMillan 1996

Greg Malouf: *Arabesque*
Publisher: Hardie Grant 2002 (first published 1999)

Mike Robinson: *Wild Flavours*
Publisher: Cassell 2005

Claudia Roden: *A Book of Middle Eastern Food*
Publisher: Penguin 1968

Anne Willan: *French Regional Cooking*
Publishers: Hutchinson and Co. Ltd. 1981

INDEX

A

armagnac

asparagus

avocado

B

bacon

basil

beans

beef